EARTHLY LOVE

STORIES OF INTIMACY AND DEVOTION

from

ORION
MAGAZINE

FOREWORD BY
BARRY LOPEZ

Published by *Orion* magazine.
All essays appeared in *Orion* or *Orion* books.

© 2020 *Orion* Magazine

Orion
1 Short Street
Northampton, MA 01060
orionmagazine.org

Editor-in-Chief: H. Emerson Blake
Creative Director: Madeline Miller
Editors: Kathleen Yale and Sumanth Prabhaker
Managing Editor: Tara Rae Miner
Design: Hans Teensma | Impressinc.com

Thanks to Sonali Zohra for illustrating the Kickstarter campaign for this book. And many thanks to the four hundred people who donated through Kickstarter and directly to *Orion* to help make this book possible.

ISBN: 978-0-913098-00-4

Printed in Canada

Dedicated to Brian Doyle

TABLE OF CONTENTS

FOREWORD

Love in a Time of Terror

BARRY LOPEZ

This world is just a little place, just the red in the sky,
before the sun rises, so let us keep fast hold of hands,
that when the birds begin, none of us be missing.
— Emily Dickinson, in a letter, 1860

SOME YEARS before things went bad, I arrived in an Aboriginal settlement called Willowra, in Australia's Northern Territory. A small village, it's haphazardly situated on the east bank of the Lander River, a dry watercourse. (I'd driven into the area several days before with a small team of restoration biologists. They were intent on reintroducing a small marsupial in the vicinity, the rufous hare-wallaby [*Lagorchestes hirsutus*, or *mala* in the local language]. The animal had been eliminated locally by feral house cats, domestic pets left behind decades before by white settlers.) When I arrived in Willowra, I was introduced to several Warlpiri people by a friend of mine, an anthropologist named Petronella

Vaarzon-Morel. She'd been working for some years around Willowra and when the biologists dropped me off—that work now completed—she helped move me into a residence in the settlement, a guesthouse where she had been living. Petra then returned to her home in Alice Springs and I was on my own.

Before she left, Petra had pointed out numerous places in the countryside nearby that I should neither approach nor show any interest in. These were mostly innocuous-looking spots to my eye —rocks, trees, small sand hills—but they were important elements in the Dreamtime narratives that form the foundation of Warlpiri identity. Many of these sites were close to the Lander. When I asked my hosts, then, if I might walk out into the desert a few miles, in the direction that I was indicating, and then return along roughly the same track, the man I was speaking to pointed in a slightly different direction and said simply, "Maybe better."

I set off that afternoon on a walk north and west of the village, across a rolling spinifex plain that stretched away to hills on the horizon in almost every direction. The flow of the bland, uniform colors of the countryside was only broken up by an occasional tree or a copse of trees.

This universe of traditional Warlpiri land was completely new to me. I had no anxiety, however, about getting lost out there. At a distance of several miles, the settlement and the Lander, with its tall gallery forest of gum trees growing along its banks, remained prominent, in a land that displayed to my cultural eyes no other real prominences.

It was midday when I left so if I happened to walk too far to the west (on what would soon be a moonless night in June) darkness might conceivably force me to lie down and wait for dawn. (I could easily have strayed unawares into some broad, shallow depression on that plain, from which all horizons would appear identical.) But getting lost seemed most unlikely. Starlight alone, in this sparsely populated country lying on the southern border of another, much more stark, challenging, and enormous desert, the Tanami, would be enough to guide me home.

My goal that day was intimacy—the tactile, olfactory, visual, and sonic details of what, to most people in my culture, would appear to be a wasteland. This simple technique of awareness had long been my way to open a conversation with any unfamiliar landscape. Who are you? I would ask. How do I say your name? May I sit down? Should I go now? Over the years I'd found this way of approaching whatever was new to me consistently useful: establish mutual trust, become vulnerable to the place, then hope for some reciprocity and perhaps even intimacy. You might choose to handle an encounter with a stranger you wanted to get to know better in the same way. Each person, I think, finds their own way into an unknown world like this spinifex plain; we're all by definition naive about the new, but unless you intend to end up alone in your life, it seems to me you must find some way in a new place—or with a new person—to break free of the notion that you can be certain of what or whom you've actually encountered. You must, at the very least, establish a truce with realities not your own, whether you're speaking about the innate truth and aura of a landscape or a person.

I've felt for a long time that the great political questions of our time—about violent prejudice, global climate change, venal greed, fear of the Other—could be addressed in illuminating ways by considering models in the natural world. Some consider it unsophisticated to explore the nonhuman world for clues to solving human

dilemmas, and wisdom's oldest tool, metaphor, is often regarded
with wariness, or even suspicion in my culture. But abandoning
metaphor entirely only paves the way to the rigidity of fundamen-
talism. To my way of thinking, to prefer to live a metaphorical
life — that is, to think abstract problems through on several planes
at the same time, to stay alert for symbolic and allegorical mean-
ings, to appreciate the utility of nuance — as opposed to living a
literal life, where most things mean in only one way, is the norm
among traditional people like the Warlpiri, in my experience. In
listening to negotiations, for example, between representatives of
industrialized societies and representatives of traditional societies, it has always seemed to me that the latter presentation is
meant to be more open to interpretation (in order not to become
trapped in literalness), while the former presentation too often
defaults to logic and "impressive" data sets, but, again, perhaps
this is only me.

The goal in these conversations, from a traditional point of view,
is to put off for a good while arriving at any conclusion, to continue
to follow, instead, several avenues of approach until a door no one
had initially seen suddenly opens. My own culture — I don't mean
to be overly critical here — tends to assume that while such conversations should remain respectful, the outcome had to conform to
what my culture considers "reality."

My point here is that walking off into what was for me anonymous territory, one winter afternoon in north-central Australia, was
not so much an exercise in trying to improve myself as a naturalist
as it was an effort to divest myself of the familiar categories and
hierarchies that otherwise might guide my thoughts and impres-
sions of the place.

I wanted to open myself up as fully as I could to the possibility of loving this place, in some way; but to approach that goal, I had first to come to know it. As is sometimes the case with other types of aquaintanceships, to suddenly love without really knowing is to opt for romance, not commitment and obligation.

The evening before I went off to explore the desert around Willowra, I finished a book called *The Last of the Nomads* by William John Peasley, published in 1983. Peasley recounts here a journey he made into the Gibson Desert in Western Australia with four other white men in the winter of 1977. They were accompanied by an Aboriginal man named Mudjon. The group was looking for two Mandildjara people believed to be the last of the Mandildjara living in the bush. Mudjon, a Mandildjara elder living at the time in a settlement on the western edge of the Gibson called Wiluna, had known for decades both of the people they were searching for — a hunter, Warri Kyango, and his wife, Yatungka Kyango. These two had refused to "come in" to Wiluna with the last of the Mandildjara people during a prolonged drought in the seventies. Mudjon respected their effort to continue living a traditional life under these very formidable circumstances but he feared that at their ages — Warri was sixty-nine, Yatungka sixty-one — they were getting too old to make their way successfully in the outback without the help of other, younger people.

The search for this couple, across hundreds of square miles of parched, trackless country, interrupted in various places by areas of barren sand hills, culminated with the party's finding the couple, together with their dingos, at a place called Ngarinarri. (The dingos helped them hunt and huddled up close with them on cold nights to share their warmth.) A few palmfuls of muddy water every day from a seep, and a small store of fruit from a nearby stand of quandong trees, was all that was sustaining them. Warri was injured and sick, and they were both emaciated.

An argument later ensued in Wiluna and then spread far and wide about the insistence of the rescue party that the couple travel with them back to Wiluna instead of leaving them there to die at Ngarinarri, which it seemed they preferred to "civilized" life in Wiluna.

I wasn't party to this, of course, so can offer no judgment, but this is an old story, characterizing many encounters over the years between "civilized" and traditional styles of living in the Australian bush. Like many readers, I brooded over the fate of these people for days after reading the book. (They both passed away within a year of their arrival in Wiluna, despite the availability there of food, water, and medical treatment.) This is a story of injustice, of course, and, too, a tragedy that virtually anyone can understand. What really stuck in my mind, though, was how love dramatized this narrative, a narrative as profound in its way as the other narrative, the one about colonial indifference and enduring harm.

Because Warri and Yatungka were both born into the same moiety among the Mandildjara, they were prevented by social custom from marrying. When they defied this custom and married anyway, their lives from then on, after their formal banishment, became far more difficult. They knew if they attempted to return to the society of their own people, they risked being physically punished. So they chose a life on their own. Even when they learned, years later, that they had been forgiven, and that their Mandildjara culture was unraveling further in the face of colonial intrusion, and even though they learned that a terrible period of widespread drought had brought most all of the "desert tribes" into white settlements like Wiluna, they continued to choose their marriage and their intimately known traditional country.

Warri and Yatungka looked after each other over all that time, and they took care of their beloved country according to the prescriptions and proscriptions in the Dreamtime stories, observing their obligations to it. They also knew, I have to think, that the watering places their people had traditionally depended on for generations had now withered and dried up or, in the case of the animals they regularly hunted, their food had simply departed the country. And yet they refused to succumb, even at what you might call the point of their natural end. It would be arrogant and certainly perilous to subscribe to any theory of what the two of them might have been thinking at the end, at Ngarinarri. What stood out for me as obvious, however, was their fierce allegiance — to their Mandildjara country and to each other. Death in this case was not for them tragic but inevitable, onerous but acceptable; and death in this place was preferable to lives lived out in Wiluna.

But, of course, again, this is not for me to determine.

The day I walked out into the desert in the direction I was pointed I was intent on immersing myself in the vastness of something I didn't know. I carried in my backpack a few books about recognizing and preparing "bush tucker," the desert plants and small creatures that could sustain Aboriginal people; a dependable bird book; and some notes about marsupials and poisonous snakes. In terms of what governed the line of my footsteps, my many changes of direction, my pauses, my squattings down, it was primarily my desire to pursue immersion — letting the place overwhelm me.

Drifting through my mind all the while, however, was the story of Warri and Yatungka, or at least the version of it that was written up and that I had read.

At some point late that day, I came upon several dozen acres of land more truly empty than the desert landscape I'd been walking through for hours. It consisted of an expanse of bare ground and coarse sand with shattered bits of dark volcanic rock scattered about. I walked as carefully here as I might have through an abandoned cemetery. Silence rose from every corner of the place, and the utter lack of life here drew heavily on my heart. As I walked on, I saw no track of any animal, no windblown leaf from a mulga tree, no dormant seed waiting for rain. Other images of bleakness came to mind: bomb-shattered rubble that buried the streets of Kabul; a small island in Cumberland Sound, a part of Baffin Island in Nunavut, Canada, where dozens of large whale skeletons lay inert in acres of tawny sea grass rolling in the wind like horses' manes; the remains of a nineteenth-century whaling station; tiers of empty sleeping platforms, each bunk designed to hold four men, rising to the ceiling in a derelict barracks at Birkenau, where every night exhausted men lay in darkness, waiting to be carted off in wheelbarrows to the nearby ovens and burned on the day they could no longer wield their tools.

I had halted with these images pushing through my mind and in the moment was toeing a stone the size of my fist when another thought burst in, that most of the trouble that afflicts human beings in their lives can be traced to the failure to love.

In the summer of 1979, I traveled to an Eskimo village in the central Brooks Range in Alaska called Anaktuvuk Pass. My friend

Bob Stephenson had a sod home in this settlement of 110 Nunamiut people, and in the days following our arrival we spent many
hours listening to stories about local animals: wolverines and
snowy owls, red foxes and caribou. The Nunamiut were enthusiastically interested in their lives, as were we. We spent a few
days, too, hunting for active wolf dens in the upper reaches of
the Anaktuvuk River. Then we flew several hundred miles west
to the drainage of the Utukok River. Bob was a large-mammal
biologist with the Alaska Department of Fish and Game, and the
department maintained a temporary summer camp there on the
middle Utukok, where field biologists could regularly observe
tundra grizzlies, caribou, wolves, gyrfalcons, wolverines, and
other creatures during the summer months. Bob and I stayed a
few days with them and then helicoptered south to a place in the
De Long Mountains farther up the Utukok called Ilignorak Ridge.
We camped there for a week, watching a wolf den across the river
from us—five adults and five pups.

Whenever I'm asked what I love, I think of the aggregate of relationships in that place that summer. Twenty-four hours of sunshine
every day at 68° northern latitude. Cloudless skies, save for fair-
weather cumulus. Light breezes. No schedule for our work but our
own. Large animals present to us at almost every moment of the
day. And, this far north of the treeline, looking through a gin-clear
atmosphere with forty-power spotting scopes, we enjoyed unob-
structed views of their behavior, even when they were two or three
miles away. I had daily conversations with Bob about the varied and
unpredictable behavior of wild animals (or, as I later came to think
of them, free animals, those still undisturbed by human interfer-
ence). We reminisced about other trips we'd made together in the

years before this, on the upper Yukon River and out to St. Lawrence Island, in the northern Bering Sea.

The mood in our camp was serene, unhurried. We were excited about being alive, about our growing friendship, about this opportunity to watch free animals in good weather, and about the timelessness of our simple daily existence. I loved the intensity of our vigil. Every day we watched what was for us—probably for any-one—the most spectacular things: wolves chasing caribou; a grizzly trying to break into the wolf den, being fought off by a single young wolf; thirty caribou galloping through shallow water in the Utukok, backed by the late evening sun, thousands of flung diamonds spar-kling in the air around them; an arctic fox sitting its haunches ten yards from the tent, watching us intently for twenty minutes.

When we returned to base camp, we enjoyed meals with the other scientists and talked endlessly with them about incidents of intriguing behavior among the animals we all watched every day. One afternoon someone brought in a mammoth tusk she had dug out of a gravel bank close by. Somehow, we no longer felt we were living in the century from which we had arrived.

During those days we all resided at the heart of incomprehensible privilege.

Evidence of the failure to love is everywhere around us. To contemplate what it is to love today brings us up against reefs of darkness and walls of despair. If we are to manage the havoc—ocean acidification, corporate malfeasance and government corruption, endless war—we have to reimagine what it means to live lives that matter, or we will only continue to push on with the unwarranted hope that things will work out. We need to step into a deeper conversation about enchantment and agape, and to actively explore a greater capacity to love other humans. The old ideas—the crushing immorality of maintaining the nation-state, the life-destroying beliefs that to care for others is to be weak and that to be generous is to be foolish—can have no future with us.

It is more important now to be in love than to be in power. It is more important to bring E. O. Wilson's biophilia into our daily conversations than it is to remain compliant in a time of extinction, ethnic cleansing, and rising seas. It is more important to live for the possibilities that lie ahead than to die in despair over what has been lost.

Only an ignoramus can imagine now that pollinating insects, migratory birds, and pelagic fish can depart our company and that we will survive because we know how to make tools. Only the misled can insist that heaven awaits the righteous while they watch the fires on Earth consume the only heaven we have ever known.

The day of illumination I had in the spinifex plain west of Willowra, about a world generated by the failure to love, which was itself kindled by the story of the lovers Warri and Yatungka, grew out of my certain knowledge that, years before, I had experienced what it meant to love, on those summer days with friends in the Brooks Range. The experience delivered me into the central project of my adult life as a writer, which is to know and love what we have been given, and to urge others to do the same.

Over the four decades I have been reading *Orion*, I have felt that many of its most memorable pieces have been efforts to frame and reframe the same question: Have you loved? In the following pages you will read some of those pieces, as well as new, original essays on the inestimable power of love to pry open, to heal, to elevate, and to transport.

In this trembling moment, with light armor under several flags rolling across northern Syria, with civilians beaten to death in the streets of Occupied Palestine, with fires roaring across the vineyards of California, and forests being felled to ensure more space for development, with student loans from profiteers breaking the backs of the young, and with Niagaras of water falling into the oceans from every sector of Greenland, in this moment, is it still possible to face the gathering darkness, and say to the physical Earth, and to all its creatures, including ourselves, fiercely and without embarrassment, I love you, and to embrace fearlessly the burning world?

EARTHLY LOVE

PAM HOUSTON

For as Many Days as We Have Left

September 19, 2017

Dear Pam,

What a great morning. Cooked up some pancakes and eggs, sat down at the computer and read your wonderful e-mail! I loved it. Thank you.

I hiked into Wason Park by way of East Willow today. Oooohhhh my. What a day. The La Garitas have nourished my body with berries, mushrooms, trout, and elk over the years. Phoenix Peak is my stupa, and the willows, wind, elk, and creeks my sangha. I feel like I hear the voices of miners and woodsmen in the babble of the creeks in Phoenix and Wason Parks.

The reason I visited this area today is because I wanted to ask about you . . . about us.

What I am about to share with you is more personal, more open, than I have ever been with anyone. If this doesn't scare you away, well, then . . . let's just see what happens.

I tasted raspberries just barely hanging on to the bushes as I hiked up La Garita Stock Driveway. They were so ripe I didn't have to chew them, just suck their flesh and juice that was two parts sweet and one part tart. Then pried the seeds out from my back teeth with my tongue.

The hike was magnificent. The colors of the shrubs and forbs in the spruce were like an ever-changing kaleidoscope as I walked up the path toward Wason. My mind moved from the present moment to thoughts of you and how you would love this hike and then back to the present . . . and then back to you. You were on my mind a lot, as you should have been as I had a question to answer.

The sun was out as I broke out of the trees and worked my way up the steep alpine meadow to the edge of Wason Park. Phoenix and La Garita Peaks loomed above to the side. A snow squall hit just as I crested a hill at the edge of Wason. I saw it coming, so I was able to put on an extra layer for warmth and my raincoat and rain pants just before it hit. The winds picked up to twenty miles an hour and I was pelted with graupel. A sign for what I've been through?

I hunkered down on the lee side of the hill with Wason Park spreading out before me and ate some snacks. The squall only lasted about ten to fifteen minutes and then the sun came out again and embraced me with warmth. An elk I couldn't see bugled (really). A sign for where I am now?

I got up and walked toward the base of the peaks and photographed the willows and peaks. Another squall moved in and left. Some light clouds then covered the sun, providing great lighting for photography. I must admit, I wasn't super focused on photography, but on being present and feeling the energy build inside me as I circled back below the peaks to one side and the incredible views of Nelson Mountain and the headwaters of Whited Creek (another place dear to me) on the other. I walked along the edge of a cliff band and looked down at the jumble of boulders and strings of willow. Took a few more pics and then began to work my way back down to the creek that the stock driveway follows.

The sun broke out from behind the clouds, so I sat down next to a few widely spaced krummholz and sipped some water and ate dried fruit and nuts. I thought about you and how you have opened up to me like no one has ever done before. I thought, But does she really know how to love? How to drop all the walls? How to give and receive? How to let go of her ego? And, of course, I asked, Do I?

Then I packed up, stood up, faced Phoenix Peak looking so majestic in the sun, raised my hands toward the mountain, and breathed. With each breath, thick energy was drawn up from the ground and spread through my entire body. With each out breath, it moved back down into the ground (this is a qigong practice). I've done this many times, but the energy never felt quite as dense as today. On my last in breath, I held the energy in my body and didn't let it go. Then I put my palms together and moved my hands to my chest and asked the mountain to make us work. And a feeling of love washed over me.

The hike down was wonderful. Beauty everywhere. I couldn't stop smiling.

I hope you don't think I'm too wacko after reading this e-mail. If so, well, it is who I am and I thought you should know. Attached are a few pics from the day. Enjoy!

Mike

September 20, 2017

Dear Mike,

You know very well I don't think you are wacko. And I have been smiling so hard since I read this the first time, it is a wonder I can even type. This is the you I knew was in there—the "Phoenix Peak is my stupa and the willows, elk, and creeks my sangha" you—not that I don't also like the more stoic version; I obviously do—but what pure delight to see this rapture, your deep love for this landscape. It is such a beautiful thing. Far from scaring me off, what you have said here about these places confirms everything my heart already knew about you. How did it know? Something to do with energy. Something to do with intuition. Something, probably, to do with the mountains themselves.

Then there is the me part. The fact that you took me with you up there. And the questions you asked about me, which of course, I have been asking of myself. Which means I need to tell you another story.

This summer, I was teaching in Chamonix, France. Chamonix has some of the best energy of anyplace I have ever been. San Juan– quality energy. Mont Blanc hovers over the valley, and in June the glacier and the snow-covered dome stay lit till almost midnight, long after the valley is in darkness. And yet in spite of its size and grandeur, or maybe partly because of it, the valley has the gentlest energy. For three years in a row I have watched students come with their fears of whatever . . . writing, riding chairlifts, parasailing, telling the truth, and I watch the valley work on them, watch them expand before my eyes.

Anyway, during this, the year I have dedicated to openhearted-ness, I had many, many conversations with that mountain. I walked either on it, or on the ridge across from it every day. I asked it to teach me how to love better, how to love straight out of my heart without it getting all gummed up in my brain, how to respond to fear and insecurity and negative self-talk by doubling back and getting bigger, opening my heart wider, reaching out instead of pulling back.

Of course, it is one thing to have these conversations with a mountain, yet another to put them into practice with friends and students and colleagues, and yet another still in (romantic) love. But I could feel there in Chamonix that I was getting ready for something. I walked more than fifteen miles a day there (and taught for three hours from five to eight when I finished). On all my walks and hikes I was talking to that mountain. Asking it to teach me. I was so happy those weeks, and I couldn't even explain to myself why. It felt like being in love, except there was no person there, not even in my imagination. I think now I was teaching myself the beauty of openheartedness for its own sake. I was using the muscles, waking them up. Above all, I was promising myself that I would not lose ground on the work I had done all year to unfreeze certain parts of me that had frozen—some that had never come to life at all—only certain parts, but important ones.

So can I do all those things you asked if I could do? God, I hope so. I know I can love and I know I can give. Receiving will be less familiar but welcome, and I am so ready to try. I don't feel the need for walls in your presence. Have not from the start. I'm not saying I won't misstep. But I believe if my heart is right, you'll give me a break. I also know you weren't asking me these questions (you were asking the mountain), but these are my answers.

When I was up in Washington State and my student/friend Becky Mandelbaum came so we could give that reading together, I was telling her about you. She's working in North Cascades National Park this summer, and she spent all last winter at the ranch. Like us, she lives to be on a hiking trail. Anyhow, we were texting today and I was telling her some more stuff, and her exact text was "God, Pam, he sounds wonderful. Like the way a mountain is wonderful." And that's it exactly. You and the San Juans have exchanged so many cells over the years, you are kind of made of them. You give off the same good thing. I would tell Red Mountain anything and everything. You see what I mean about the mountains being in charge?

There are a million other things to say, but this is a start on it. What I would really like to do is drive up there and give you a giant hug (but I would be late for class in the morning). Thank you for opening your heart to me. It's a beautiful heart. I'm going to send you some photos of Mont Blanc.

Pam

If I were to try to explain to someone why, at the age of fifty-six, having sworn off romantic relationships forever, I agreed to marry a sixty-one-year-old lifer forest ranger named Mike Blakeman, I could do no better than to refer to these two e-mails. These two of hundreds of e-mails we sent in the year we were getting to know each other came relatively early in our courtship, when we had only had a few meals together, and a few brief hours walking along the river, looking for eagles in the big cottonwoods across the Rio Grande from Mike's house.

When I read the Wason Park e-mail to a few close friends, their reactions ranged from head-shaking wonder at how, after all these years I had found my match, to playful accusations of having written the letter myself. Even at the beginning it was undeniable that Mike and I not only loved, but *saw* the natural world in many of the very same ways, sometimes, it seemed, with the very same eyes.

Not long after we exchanged these particular letters, we headed up on a Forest Service road toward the Rio Grande's headwaters, my wolfhounds, William and Olivia, in the back, heads out the windows, giant tongues and ears flapping. The aspens were at their peak, and Mike brought his camera. We are both hobbyist landscape photographers, our very first conversations had been about light, pattern, and form. I was driving, and as we rolled past the hillsides, the aspen groves changing in broad swathes of tequila sunrise shades, I kept my eyes peeled for shots, the edge of a rock formation breaking the regularity of the forest, or a cluster of aspens with pleasingly hatch-marked trunks, or a curve of the road where the backlighting turned all the leaves fluorescent, clouds behind lit purple and blue from within.

"Do you want that one?" I would say, tapping the brakes, and much more often than not, Mike had seen the very same shot.

We left the living aspens and entered the scar of the West Fork Fire—109,000 acres of climate-driven char and burn. In some places new aspens were coming, in others there would only be meadow. In the U.S., every year since 2000, an average of 72,400 fires have burned an average of 7 million acres a year. In Colorado, the spruce and pine beetles have killed one in every fourteen trees, nearly a billion total trees statewide.

I held my new love up like a prism through which to view the decimated landscape. I thought about the unstable man-child who'd been put in charge of the nuclear codes, about skinny whales and dying coral, and about the government's agenda to pollute the air and water, to eliminate the Endangered Species Act. I woke up choking on grief about it every morning, and yet I was in real healthy love for the first time in my life.

Mike and I had spent the last twenty-six and forty years (respectively) cultivating a love relationship with the Eastern San Juan Mountains that surrounded our homes. Now we had been called to try and love each other the way we had learned to love the land. We were already talking about how we could take the love we had found for each other and turn it back out toward the community, to team teach an environmental education class, to create a safe haven for immigrants, to fight for wolves and bears.

A month after that day at the headwaters, Mike and I drove over to Canyonlands National Park for a weekend, camped in the Needles campground, and hiked to Chesler Park. It was mid-October by then, and the fall colors had descended from the high country to red rock canyon level. Mike had never been to Chesler Park, but it had always been one of my favorite destinations, a place my twenty-five-year-old self had said, oddly, *I would like to get married here one day*, even though my twenty-five-year-old self had absolutely zero desire to get married, then or in any future she could see. Mike took a picture of me hiking down the trail away from him with my arms extended, my palms all but brushing the tops of the chamisa on either side. I can tell just by the way I am lifting my foot to take the next step on the trail that I am absolutely as happy in that moment as I have ever been in my life.

Not far to the west of Canyonlands sit the 700,000 acres of former federally protected land Trump has opened up for oil and gas drilling, coal mining, and mineral extraction, after cutting the Grand Staircase–Escalante National Monument in half. I thought of my friend Terry Tempest Williams, and how she spent years of her life fighting for the protection of that land. My mind flashed to a photo of the two of us signing our first books together at a Salt Lake City Book Festival more than thirty years ago, looking, honestly, not drinking age between us. The smiles on our faces suggest we believed the whole natural world was out there for us to explore and love and save.

In her latest book, *Erosion*, Terry suggests the climate catastrophe we are currently entering represents a new type of challenge for humanity because, unlike previous hardships, it will not be a matter of knuckling down and getting through to the other side. The climate catastrophe has no other side, or not, anyway, for humanity, because humanity *is* the hardship that must be gotten through. Very few (if any) humans will be around to take the measure of whether the Earth lives or dies at our hands, and in the biggest picture, that may be the good news. E. O. Wilson says we could take Earth all the way down to the microbes and she would still find a way to recover. Once we recognize ourselves as Earth's destroyer, it becomes possible to believe that once she rids herself of her most persistent parasite, she will be free to heal herself.

That December Mike and I went down to Big Bend National Park for a week and hiked the South Rim Trail in the Chisos Mountains. The South Rim is a nice long day hike, thirteen miles around and a couple thousand feet of elevation gain and loss if you take all the extensions. We took so many photos of the shadowed hills and desert badlands that extended into Mexico, we barely made it back to the campground before winter's early dark. We drank sotol out of a cloudy plastic milk crate with some kids from Mesilla, New Mexico, and shared with them the lamb stew Mike had cooked up at home and frozen into ice blocks for the trip. The next morning, we followed the Rio Grande as far as we could into Santa Elena Canyon, listened to our voices echo off the golden walls, and hiked across parched desert to a spring erupting with butterflies.

We talked about the children, lonely and sick and dying in cages to the east and the west of us along the border, of Trump's vanity wall that would rip through that fragile ecosystem with no regard for all the wild creatures that migrated back and forth for food or forage or drink.

Before humans arrived on Earth, there'd been less than one extinction per millennium. Now we were losing two species a decade—mammals, even, most recently a bat and a rat. How do we continue to love the earth and each other inside the knowledge that humans are driving the sixth extinction? And because all love begins with the ability to love the self, how do we accomplish that when we are, each of us, culpable in the earth's demise? How do we rest easy in the face of our own rampant consumerism, and even if we choose to live simply—to eat a diet heavy in vegetables, install solar panels, waste no food, and drive an electric car—how do we sleep at night when we have a president who is doing everything he can to accelerate the disaster primarily because of how much he feels inferior to a moral and dignified black man?

The next summer, when Mike and I got married, it didn't rain at all. For the first time in our twenty-five years of living at the ranch, the pasture saved itself by staying dormant and I had to buy hay all summer. The trees that hadn't burned in the West Fork Fire were stressed by the lack of moisture, making them more susceptible to the remaining spruce beetles and other climate-driven disease. We waited for fire, which came to many places near us, but not to our valley per se. I'd been working on putting the ranch into a conservation easement and I went ahead with it, knowing it would appraise far lower than it would have if the pastures were their normal summer lush. I watered a tiny piece of the yard so my geriatric horse could eat some sweet grass on his very last summer on Earth. The only wedding gift I wanted was a rainstorm.

We began the ceremony at noon, and by ten the big black clouds we hadn't seen all summer were gathering over the divide. As I vowed to be Mike's partner *in whatever small or large way we might work to help this heartbroken country and the people and animals and wild things most at risk in the time of climate change and fascism,* thunder boomed over Mt. Baldy. The first drops of rain hit just as we all scooted inside the big white tent, me wishing I had paid extra for the optional removable third and fourth sides.

It rained so long and so hard while we ate our beautiful wedding feast that a few of our friends went out in their Sunday clothes and dug a ditch around the tent to keep the dance floor from flooding. It was the only significant rain event of the summer and coincided almost exactly with the four-hour reception. There was no doubt in my mind it was a blessing, but for what task, exactly, were we being blessed? Loving each other? Loving the land? Was it a friendly reminder from Mother Nature that we had only *ever* had the present moment to love, to kiss, to dance in the rain, even before the end had seemed so imminent? Perhaps it was an imperative to hold the wonder of our love for each other and the San Juan Mountains in one hand and our grief for a billion Colorado trees, drought-starved elephants, and a third of all birds that have disappeared from North America in our lifetimes in the other.

Our first anniversary took us to Iceland, where the glacier, Okjökull (Icelanders called it, affectionately, OK), had recently become the first in that country to go extinct. Icelanders held a funeral for OK at the site, planted a plaque to mourn its loss, to record the date and the parts per million of carbon dioxide in the air at the time of the ceremony: 415. The plaque read: *OK is the first Icelandic Glacier to lose its status as a glacier. In the next 200 years all our glaciers are expected to follow the same path. This monument is to acknowledge that we know what is happening and what needs to be done. Only you know if we did it.* In the pristine Westfjords, the Norwegians were farming salmon, a deal the government made that locals said was almost sure to decimate the local fisheries; the nets and tenders were in nearly every single fjord.

All that said, it was not hard to find parts of Iceland that were wild and clean and untrammeled. We also discovered that all over the country, steps that lead to the doors of churches have been painted with rainbow stripes. Per capita plastic use in Iceland is a fraction of what it is in the U.S.; when you go to the grocery store, you have two choices of yogurt, or crackers, or chocolate, instead of 102.

We chose Iceland as a destination because it had been declared number one on the Global Peace Index since 2008, and because we were exhausted by the gun and rape culture of the U.S., which ranked 128 (and falling fast) out of 163 in 2019. The commitment to sustainability in Iceland, the clean air and water, felt like a kind of freedom we will never know again in the U.S. If we could come here once a year, we told each other, for a month or maybe two, we might recover some semblance of hope or happiness, some ease about the way we walked on the earth. But even as we said the words, we recognized that maybe unfettered hope and happiness were exactly what got us to the disaster we are now facing. And that by taking those airplanes back and forth and back to Iceland, we would hasten the death of whatever Icelandic glacier is next on the chopping block, and that Iceland should not be made to suffer because our own country has become a place we can no longer find hope for peace.

When you get married at fifty-six and sixty-one, you quickly discover, the words *to have and to hold forever* take on a slightly different cast. In no scenario is our love going to get enough time to fully blossom, so it's imperative not to sweat the small stuff, to drop the walls *and* the ego, to make the most of every single day. Mike and I built our love for each other from our love of the forests and mountains and meadows. Can our love endure if every tree burns, if the air gets so full of methane that wildflowers can't grow, if nothing is left for elk and bears to eat on the hillsides? If loving the landscape taught us how to love each other, can loving each other help us bear the loss of landscapes we love, or does it elevate the pain exponentially? And once all the wilderness has been destroyed, once every living thing has been extracted and consumed, does our love become a memorial, some kind of hologram of all the things that used to be? When you get married at fifty-six and sixty-one, you quickly discover, the answer to all of the questions are yes.

In the middle of writing this essay, I texted Mike the question "what does it mean to love another person in a dying world?" He was in Colorado, and I was in California. He texted back: *Love provides respite from the suffering? Grounds one in the present instead of dwelling in the fear of the future? Provides a feeling of safety even as everything falls apart? Moving forward toward the danger together? There's the difficult emotion that humans are driving this sixth extinction, but there is also the understanding that life will go on without us. Take yourself outside, my sweet, and look up at the moon and the stars.*

Sometimes, when I lie in bed at the ranch, the Milky Way bright outside the bedroom window, my head on Mike's chest, listening to his heartbeat, I think, okay, let it end now . . . now . . . now . . . I am where I belong and I am ready. But not one of us is going to get out of here that easy; none of us is going to get out without bearing witness to suffering on a scale that this decade's fires and floods are only beginning to reveal.

Who will be the last humans on Earth? How many will survive the climate-driven wars, the drought, storms, fires and floods, death of the bees, and the end of agriculture? What will those people have learned about love? What will they have learned about greed and cooperation?

One thing I do know is that as our suffering gets greater, so must our love. Not just me and Mike, not just one for another, but all of us, for all of us, and for Earth in distress. What is left for us is to walk into the devastation awake and full of compassion.

We are going to have to love fiercely, and fervently, all the way to the end, with nothing to protect us but our empathy, our sensitivity, our mercy, and our courage. Love at the end of the world must not be a diminished love, but one of endless expansion.

Outside the bedroom window, the stars sparkle their near infinity and in that too is respite.

"What's the name of that one again?" comes Mike's sleepy voice in my ear.

"That's the Pleiades," I said, "the seven sisters. Orion was in love with all of them. See how he's chasing them across the sky?"

"I don't need seven sisters," Mike says, and I tell him I am glad to hear it.

"I need you," he says, "for exactly as many days as we have left."

JEAN MONAHAN

The Kiss

We've been saying something like this
For months: slow-ripened sounds
Wafting out of our mouths the way
The hot sweet sweat of cut hay
Whispers and lifts out of a noon field;
Setting each other in our sights
The way the black and white and staring eye
Of the egret fishes: with precision,
Interpreting the light, the ridged waves,
The streaked and mottled back of the catch;
Leaning nearer, close enough to watch
The beloved vein in the neck fire, see
Salt on the lip, the whole forest smoking
As the meteorite burns a swath.
I tell you now, the glacier may take years
To advance, but it never stops moving.
The eyes of the wolf are bigger
And hungrier than we remember.
Look at how my mouth yearns toward yours.
The next conversation, we will speak in tongues.

MARK SCHIMMOELLER

Untitled

You lay your smile over me
like the sprawl of blackberry thickets
on the sloping ridge, berries
dropping into
an empty milk jug,
as wind into a sail—I'm drifting after
an old scattering of seeds. Your smile
is that big. It grows oak,
sumac, wild rose, tulip poplar on this
upturned terrain.

I find blackberry boughs hooked onto
high limbs, fruiting
without sun. Blackberries are fewer here,
but huge (shade is an act
of forgetting), the air bruised
by seed loaded, high-
dangling fruit.

LAUREL NAKANISHI

A Private Wild

Out beyond male and female, gay and straight,
there are mountains

I T WAS STILL winter in Montana when we crunched through icy
snow, its powder packed down by couples and families, solo
walkers and bands of teenagers. This was a popular trail, flat
and beautiful and only a couple of miles outside of town. Usually
we would meet crowds of other hikers, but on that day, perhaps because of the late hour or the flurries of gentle snow, we were alone.

In my flimsy, sheepskin boots, I was underprepared for this hike
and slushy weather. The soles were soft, and I could feel myself
slipping a little with each step. I already felt off-balance: beside me
Caley walked with her hands in her pockets. The snow and gray-
layered sky held us in; they made for us a small, intimate space,
and we carried it with us through the sparse forest of Doug fir and
bare tamaracks. The trail dipped close to Rattlesnake Creek. To our
left a wall of gray-green basalt rose up. I could see the veins of the
rock, angling down. The stream echoed off the wall, and I thought:
*There is another secret stream deep within the stone; it is rushing and
crashing through its own dark crevice.*

Caley pushed her sandy brown hair from her face. For as long as
I'd known her, she had worn her hair in a low ponytail, with a wisp

tucked behind each ear, framing a face that was both chipper and earnest, playful and concerned. I found that I loved to talk to her about issues in the world, in our families, in our days. She laughed when others would become angry or annoyed. Her tennis shoes were full of snow! My boots were soaked, and my socks dyed my feet purple! With Caley, this was hilarious.

Suddenly, she veered off the trail and up a snowbank.

"What are you doing?" I asked.

"Come on!" She tromped up to a tree with puzzle-piece bark— later I learned it was a ponderosa pine. I watched as she placed her hands on either side of the trunk and leaned in, as if into the body of a lover. She pressed her face into the cobbled bark, then arched her back and peered up into the tall branches.

"What are you doing?"

"Smell it," she said.

I followed her footprints up the bank, trying not to slip. She stood next to the trunk smiling, almost laughing. Her nose was red from the cold, her eyes blue against her pale face. I pressed my own face into the bark and smelled vanilla, rough and sweet. Even though the air stung my nose, I breathed in again. Her face was close to mine. Suddenly, I thought of kissing her. I was surprised and embarrassed by this new thought, but there it was, and it stayed with me. I could feel the heat of her body near mine, her hair against my cheek. I kept my nose to the trunk and breathed.

I was always a tomboy. My first childhood kiss was with my best friend, Jess. We were under the belief that it was physically impossible for two girls to kiss. We had never seen it done before. Maybe girl lips just didn't fit together in the same way, we wondered.

Or perhaps they repelled like wrong-sided magnets.

One day, when we were about eight years old, we decided to try it. When we successfully pecked each other on the lips, we proudly demonstrated the kiss to our parents. "Look Mom! Muah! It *is* possible!" I don't remember what happened after that. Was my father alarmed? Did her mother scold us? Did our brothers run away shrieking?

Someone must have said something because we never did it again.

Homophobia is something I learned with Jess as well. Her mother, a home nurse at the time, was working for a gay couple, one of whom had AIDS. Jess must have overheard her parents talking about these men, or maybe her mother whispered to her over dinner the horrifying possibility: *two men, together, gay.* The next day, Jess made up a new term with which to mock our brothers: "Gaylord." We sang it out to them; we shouted it spitefully. We taunted "Gaylord! Gaylord!" until my mother made us stop. We did not really know what "gay" meant or why it was so bad. No one taught us to hate, but that was the air we were breathing.

Later in my life, my mother admitted that she had often wondered if I was gay. "It's not bad or anything," she said. "It is just such a hard life. I didn't want that for you."

But nothing was hard about being with Caley. When we were together, she made me feel safe and confident. For three years, Caley worked as a backcountry ranger in the Eastern Sierras. During the season, she camped by herself near a lake. She kept her food in a large barrel half-buried in the ground (to deter black bears). During the day she would walk the trails, answer hikers' questions, and make sure they were obeying the wilderness rules: no cutting down trees, no camping within one hundred feet of a lake or meadow, and no shortcutting trails.

In these years, Caley developed an ease with the chores and patterns of living outside society: making potable water, keeping food away from animals, dealing with weather, and navigating unknown terrain. As a novice yet enthusiastic backpacker, I found all this quite attractive.

What was most attractive, though, was her deep love for wilderness. She lit up in the mountains; she filled with wonder in the forest; she came alive among lichen-speckled boulders. Whenever we passed into a designated wilderness area, she would kiss the sign. Wilderness for her was more than just a land management label: it was a place of deep spiritual encounter.

After I had moved around some furniture in my mind ("Really, I can kiss women?!") and Caley and I began dating, I noticed how defined my gender conditioning was. I saw it in subtle physical exchanges, like waiting for Caley to take my hand in hers, or how I sought to make my body smaller, to fit myself into her embrace.

Looking back on my relationships with men, I noticed that I was gentler with their feelings. I would defer to their preferences. "No, dear, what would *you* like to do tonight?" Often, instead of saying what I wanted or needed, I would take my cues from them.

In some ways, being in a homosexual relationship was like being in the wilderness. I have been a student of heterosexual relationships all my life, witnessing my parents and my grandparents; I learned models for heterosexual relationships on television, in movies, from friends and books. But I had no clear rules about how to interact in a homosexual relationship, and within this blank space—this wild space—Caley and I could create our own ways of interacting. We played around with gender. We led and followed. We found delight in this in-between space.

One day, during the winter we met, I remember standing in line with Caley at our university's ski gear rental shop, giving my height and weight. When the student-worker went to pick out the right cross-country skis for me, Caley laughed.

"I'm bigger than you!"

"No, you're not!" I said, looking her up and down. We were both the same slight build.

"Yes, look," she said, and walked up behind me to compare our boots. We were not dating yet and her closeness felt electric, unsettling. "I'm a size bigger."

And I realized it might be true. She definitely had more muscle, which became apparent when we began our ski across the icy, late-season snow at Lolo Pass. She zoomed ahead, all confidence and grace.

When we stopped for lunch, Caley sliced cheese and then apples with her camping knife, assembling little sandwiches all along her thigh.

"My hands are cold," I said, hoping she would hold them. Hoping she would make a little cave with her own hands and blow life and feeling into my numb fingers. Instead, she offered me her gloves.

Caley and I fell in love in the wilderness and in the space away from culture that wilderness provides. In a way, despite its physical dangers, wilderness also suggests a safe space, a free space, a space of endless possibilities. In the wilderness, no one cares who I am kissing.

I remember standing in a forest of tamarack, in early spring, in western Montana, near Piegan Glacier. High in the branches, clutches of needles sprouted the color of parakeets. The grove was old, so old that the trees grew giant and mossy. They had lived in this valley for more than 150 years. I leaned against a stump where Caley sat. No one was looking at my body and Caley's body. No one was wondering what we were doing holding hands, our fingers interlaced. There, in the wilderness, there was no need for words like *lesbian* or *queer* or *bisexual*. There was no need for any labels at all.

Piegan Glacier is on land that's labeled as wilderness: a place that is supposed to be "untrammeled" by humans and human civilization. The glacier itself once covered more than sixty acres, and it's been frozen for millennia. But when we finally crested the pass and looped around to the north side of the mountain, we found only a field of dirty snow, dripping into a little stream. Climate change had melted the ice that had been frozen for thousands of years. It was a reminder that there is no great escape from ourselves. Not even in wilderness, not even with Caley.

Like our pollution, we bring parts of our culture here, too. Matthew Shepard, Gwen Araujo, the Pulse nightclub shooting in Orlando—so many of the stories I hear about queer people are violent and sad. And although I know that many queer families are living happily in communities around the country, I find that more often, I carry the violence with me—as fear, self-hate, distrust. I carry it even to the tops of melted glaciers.

The next morning, Caley and I awoke to a storm spilling from the east, shaking our tent, pocking the ground with rain, thawing ice from the lake. In this strange gray world, the green needles of the tamaracks were almost too bright. The trunks, we knew, were crowded with rings so close, they appeared as one long year. And maybe that is what wilderness has taught me: that my separate self collapses into a larger time. I am part of a grander ecosystem—an interconnected natural world that is larger than our individual cultures and human civilization.

Here in the United States, we are told that we may venture into the wilderness and find our truest selves. I am not sure if this is true, but I have found the wilderness seeping into me, working its way into my consciousness and how I see my place in the world. I like to think there is a kind of harmony available to us humans—a way to live deeply within our ecosystems. I like to think it is still possible to let mountains fill our eyes and for our bodies to be carved in glacier lines. I like to think that if I just pay attention enough, if I am humble enough, if I open myself, that this union is possible.

Soon and all too quickly, summer was ending. The hillsides were covered in red and yellow paintbrush, white poofs of bear grass and sprigs of purple lupine. We climbed the rocky, switchbacking trail to Sapphire Lake—a dot of clear water in the craggy pocket of a mountain. In the distance, a brittle creek sounded. We held in our backpacks and in our bodies a culture that was ours. We breathed in the changing climate. But, Caley still ran her fingers over the fuzzy petals of the paintbrush blooms, as if they could mark her hand with that dusty red.

Natalie Diaz

Wolf OR-7

When he left his pack to find a mate, Oregon's
seventh collared wolf, named OR-7 by state biologists,
became the first wolf in California since 1927, when
the last one was killed for government bounty.

On a digital map, OR-7's trek is charted — by a GPS
tracking collar and numerous trail cameras — a trembling
blue line,

south, west, south again,
twelve-hundred miles from Oregon to California
> to find Her: *Gray wolf, Canis lupus, Loba, Beloved.*

In the moonstruck dusk I go a same wilding path, pulled
by night's map into the forests and dunes of your hips,

divining from you rivers, then crossing them —
proving the long thirst I'd wander to be sated by you.

> I confuse instinct for desire — isn't *bite* also *touch*?

Some things cannot be charted—
the middle-night cosmography of your moving hands,

the constellation holding the gods
of your jaw and ear.

      You tell me you take wolf naps, and I turn lupanar.

A female gray wolf's shoulders are narrower than a male's,
but our mythos of shoulders began before I knew that,

      when I broke open my mouth upon yours

as we pressed against the glass doors of the cliff house
looking out into the bay's shadows hammering

      the bronzed bell of the supermoon.

My mind climbed the rise, fall, rise of your bared back.
In me a pack of wolves appeared and disappeared

      over the hill of my heart,

I, too, follow toward where I am forever-returning—
Her.

And somewhere in the dark
of a remote night-vision camera,

      the glowed green music of animals.

DAVID TOMAS MARTINEZ

Fractal

the second time
i was married
it was after three
weeks of drinking
wine chased
by hurricanes she
is so damn hot
i thought i mean
warm & exotic
so damn loving
i said inside the
eye of a storm
light refracts turns
every thing upside
down marriage is
a natural disaster
a speakeasy is
no different than
a watering hole
it propagates the
species because

so much of nature
stays exposed
we cover ourselves
initially love is a test
of vision trying to
love someone in
to loving you
we call this sight
we calm this sight
we call it serenity
carpe diem i do
everything like it
is the first time
when coupled i am
both the night owl
& the plucked fowl
with perfect vision
i can see myself
courting hitched like
talons to a mouse

ROBERT MICHAEL PYLE

Carnal Knowledge

I HAD REAL COMPUNCTION about dispatching them in the depth of their passion. They were beautiful—utterly merged—and they were stunning in their sheer physical exuberance. But letting them live would have serious consequences, as I had learned bitterly once before.

It was some fifteen years ago that I came upon a courting pair of the great gray beasts, the first I'd ever seen. I recognized them from their handsomely spotted hides, and remembered what I had read about their astonishing sexual behavior. So I placed the creatures in a terrarium to watch them. But they escaped post-coitus, and our home precincts have been populated with their voracious offspring ever since.

I am speaking of *Limax maximus*, arguably the handsomest of the large, shell-less land mollusks. Sleekly proportioned, kitten-gray, symmetrically mottled with dramatic black spots, and enormous—sometimes exceeding six inches—the leopard slug is an animal whose beauty must appeal to even the most fastidious slime-o-phobe. If only it were native! But, like the black and rusty *Arion ater*, which gobbles the garden in its teeming thousands, *L. maximus* originated in Europe. It is one of hundreds of alien species which, having coevolved with humans over many thousands of

years in the Old World, proved preadapted for disturbed habitats in
North America. So this striking animal is despised as the starling
of the slugs, no more loved than the exotic zebra mussels that clog
our waterways.

Slugs have a hard enough time with their public relations, but
when they are as devastating on the garden as this large herbivore,
they haven't a chance at mercy, even from a sympathetic naturalist. Even still, *Limax maximus* practices one of the most dramatic
sexual unions I know, thereby seducing our reluctant attention.
Like other slugs, the species is hermaphroditic. Every adult both
receives and donates spermatozoa, a lifestyle that might be considered highly progressive. But they do not gather in knots of two
or three individuals to fuse gonads among the leaf litter as does
A. ater. Nor do they engage in mutual penetration with mammoth
penises as our indigenous banana slugs do. Instead, great gray
garden slugs have contrived a copulatory routine so Byzantine as to
raise the most jaded eyebrows.

And raise is the right verb, for these slugs begin their union by
climbing a tree trunk or a wall to a high point, then circling for an
hour or more, mutually caressing with their tentacles, nipping, and
secreting copious gummy mucous. Then, gluing a sticky launch-
ing pad to the surface, they drop into the abyss on a shared bungee
cord of congealed slime. (One of the greatest attributes of mollusk
mucous is that it can be slick as greased glass one second, sticky as
superglue the next—an engineering feat no laboratory has successfully duplicated.) There the lovers dangle, like two climbers moved
to merge in mid-belay.

Such was what we beheld on a recent midnight, upon going out
to the back porch to feed the cats. Ever since that first experiment

in voyeurism and the subjects' consequent escape, *L. maximus* has
frequented our porch and the adjacent gardens. To their detriment
and the cats' patent disgust, they come to the cat food more faithfully than to any slugbait but beer. However, these two fine leopards
were sliding up the wall of the house above the cat food dish, more
intent on sex than kibbles. We decided to let them reach the ceiling
and bungee away, certain we could contain them after witnessing
the act. They made remarkable progress in their eagerness. When
we checked a few minutes later, they were already slung and linked,
their cables pasted to the clapboard wall, their embrace suspended
just above the dish. And there stood Firkin the cat, peacefully
munching, completely oblivious to the sex play unfurling inches
above her head.

The strand hung some three feet, roping the lovers upside
down. They wrapped around each other in a double helix so
intertwined that we stiff bony vertebrates could only regard their
full-body wrap with envy and awe. They dangled and spun, first this
way, then that, as their soft exertions spiraled their gyre. And all the
while their extruded milky penis sacs — half their total length —
pushed out behind their heads, mingling in a clot of blending
zygotes. First palmlike, then feathery, these creneled genitals
pulsated and throbbed like sea jellies swimming together: stroking,
dancing, fanning, swelling — finally forming a sheltering parasol as
climax overcame them.

After an hour or so, we humans were exhausted. I'd have left
matters there, but I remembered last time, and the ensuing years
of heavy plant predation. So I took the copulating leopards by their
magical harness, laid them gently in a bread bag, and placed them
in the freezer alongside a few dozen *Arion ater*. Later they will

enrich the compost, and their magnificence return to the garden of which it is made. Though they would have frozen naturally in a few weeks, making slugsicles gave me no pleasure and some sharp misgivings. Yet allowing aggressive alien species to reproduce means giving up on native species, as well as the garden. So we make our choices: *Limax* or lettuce, leopards or bananas. I console myself with the thought that there are worse ways to go than entering the Big Sleep in a state of utter rapture.

MARY ROSE O'REILLEY

The Plain Speech

After twenty years the love we make
we braid into the hair of the day.
Sometimes I watch each stitch in the quilt

white hairs pecking the days out,
sometimes I cry and stop you
to talk about death. Still you start

telling your beads of memory
into my hand. *That day*
next to the slough you say

we napped in the car. Buffalo cows
stepped out of the rocks, stopped the calves
in a half-circle behind us. We could not move

or turn. They loomed at us out of the mirrors.
You wrap me in this story, a man coming home
coat full of red cyclamen. Clay strung to the roots.

After some struggle to find the true north of their lives
great and small wings return. White-throated sparrow
slow beat of cranes crossing Dakota. Orioles take

fruit we have left on a human plate. Like a farmer
suppressing his muscles for church, behind you
the uncurtained window, beside you the iron bed

you stand in your black pants, shirtsleeves,
a patch of wrinkles smelling of damp and the iron.
You call to me in the plain speech we use at home.

Answer me *earth, mercy.*
Answer me *rain.*

A. R. Ammons

Love Song

Like the hills under dusk you
fall away from the light:
you deepen: the green
light darkens
and you are nearly lost:
only so much light as
stars keep
manifests your face:
The total night in
myself raves
for the light along your lips.

KATRINA VANDENBERG

On Cold-Weather Vegetables

GNARLED SWEET POTATOES, tips curling like the feet of witches. Hubbard squashes, big enough to sit on, warty, *blue*. Mushrooms flaring their gills. Back in July, the tomatoes and corn the farmers offered were cheery, Crayola-bright. October is scary: it holds out every child's most despised vegetable in its wrinkled claw.

Cold-weather vegetables are demanding. They require a little muscle behind the knife, and their hard shells can't be sliced as much as hacked at. Inside, their flesh is richly colored and dense. They're messy: *eviscerate* is the word that best describes how we scrape stringy flesh and seeds from a pumpkin to ready it for carving. We wrestle with them. They refuse the ease of the salad bowl and insist on a long roasting.

They are either bitter (brussels sprouts, kale) or, in the case of the roots, sweeter than the uninitiated might expect. They're acquired tastes, ones I didn't love until I was in my thirties, my husband an even more reluctant convert than I. But this time of year and at this time in our lives, our meals together are changing.

When the air begins to bite with cold and the smell of decaying leaves, the colors and tastes of what we eat begin to deepen.

I watch my husband from the kitchen window as he pulls dead morning glory vines from the trellises. I love him differently than I did the day I married him. In the fifteen years we have been together, I have helped bury his father, he has cleaned up my vomit, we have both been bored by stories we've heard dozens of times. We have lost two pregnancies. Two falls ago, in one five-week stretch, we were each separately taken to the emergency room in an ambulance and had to start thinking about what it would mean to lose the person who has witnessed so much of our lives. Eventually, surely, one of us will be left behind.

Andre Dubus describes the meals between married couples as not mere eating but a "pausing in the march to perform an act together," a sacrament that says, "I know you will die; I am sharing food with you; it is all I can do, and it is everything." My husband and I have eaten together maybe ten thousand times, in three states, in various rentals and then our house, at the same oak trestle table. Watching us, you could chronicle changes — I quit vegetarianism, he learned to cook, we started to say grace — but the act remains.

Christians regularly take Communion, a ritually shared meal that acknowledges the mysteries of life and death, but mealtime is especially poignant in the fall, when Mexicans celebrate the Day of the Dead, and Celts once celebrated Samhain, and ancient Greeks told the story of Persephone disappearing into the underworld — all harvest festivals that connect sharing food with death and gratitude. So we start with what the earth has given us. We shape it into something else. Perhaps there are candles. We talk. We have

enough and are together, even though one of us will someday eat
here alone.

The vegetables of summer are easy to love, as it is easy to find
young men and women beautiful, to promise commitment before
it has been tested, to be happy beneath a cloudless sky. I'm still
not sure it's natural to prefer what's difficult and unwieldy, to
feel affection warts-and-all. But the world is older and slower and
more patient than we ever will be. These vegetables keep, and have
helped every generation before ours survive long winters. They are
part of the great practice of not having what we want, but wanting
what we have, and after years of trying—of trying and trying—my
husband and I have both come to love, even crave, beets and
butternut squash, the hard vegetables of fall. We appreciate their
complexity. We find them very good.

JAMES GALVIN

Dear May Eighth

Why was the last kiss May seventh
And so shy?

Your tongue was skittish.

Your clavicle—
Door-bolt, little key,
Tendril—
Was the world's cross-tree—
Your collar bone was hot snow to touch.

I wanted to say commitment.
And so I was committed,
And so I did commit
Crimes against the immaculate.

I wanted to say decision.
And so I was decisive,
And so I did decide.

I was lost to my freedom,
Fell into stars.

Clavicle, clavichord,
Gold keys falling through me cold.

I wanted to be confused
In your heart
With landscape, solitude,
With alpine kisses.

I wanted to show you, remaining
Sequestered in themselves.
Awe of glacial kisses,
Wild, high altitude confusions of them.

You explain
The sky I spent my life under.
Why I'm eye-level
With snow-line,
Town a thousand feet down.

You explain
The bottom of the ocean
That packed up and left.

You say it's the basin that makes the sky a bay.

So this is the eighth of May—
Kisses plus one,
Or minus one, I guess.

The sunset plans its palette, its deployment.

It hasn't decided the denouement—
It's breathless . . .

Listen, Nobody's Business,
Why aren't you in love with me?

Is your overture over-subtle
Like this sunset—
White clavicle under gray thunderheads.
Cobalt throbs?

Streaky northern billows
And reds thrum into music—clavichord.

Red cliff below purples
Above peaks' azure.

Then—get this—
Red cliff
Is palindromed,
Butterflied, flayed.
In strata of lenticulars.

Rain rains down
Blue-black on earth
And sends riders, striders,
Bruisy yellow,
Blood in a stream,
Back to the eastern horizon—
Where I kissed you.

If you would wake with me
I'd know how to die.

Yours, May eighth.
Sincerely,
Man under influence of sky.

NICK NEELY

A Body of Trees

Meet the madrone, on whose skin we leave our mark

I HAD NOT EXPECTED to see all this mutilation. It would seem something of a tradition. Along this trail, the slender and old madrones, each and every one, are carved with the whims of passersby, resembling the arborglyphs of lonely shepherds on aspen around the West. But do you know the madrone? It is the most human of trees. It has soft, smooth skin and often bends like a dancer twisting myriad, dryadic arms. It exfoliates as it grows, shedding translucent cinnamon curls, bursting at its seams. This tree, with the milky undercolor of a honeydew melon rind, flares from nude to satin orange to fillet red, and it sometimes deigns to grow a scaly bark, rough and gray. The quintessence of umbilical, the mother tree: madrone.

Like revelers at a tavern table, we carve into this body, peanut shells underfoot. We have nothing here if not time and keys. Walking this trail to the top of Lower Table Rock near Medford, Oregon, you climb under power lines through black oak and glossy manzanita (some little cousin, by language, family, and texture) and then the madrones take hold in the nutrient-poor soil, where they thrive and wait for fire. That's where I begin to slow, noticing these

inscriptions. Studying this proliferation of incisions. They build in
number until you can't ignore them. Is this simple graffiti or collective art? A memorial or a gallery of horrors?

As a kid in California, I was taught to call these "refrigerator
trees." Put your hand on its smooth surface, docents and teachers said. Press your cheek to it. Wrap yourself around it and feel
the chill of sap close beneath the skin. As if magnetized, we are
attracted. On this trail, we leave on them missives and sketches, the
equivalent of family photos and shopping lists. Some trees are cut
so profusely that they are unreadable, sorely disfigured. Others are
only lightly marked. With smiley faces, penises, and other likable
vulgarities. With indiscriminant scratches, the passing glance of a
fingernail.

But most of all with names and, especially, initials. We remind
these trees and ourselves of our persistence. SETH scrawled as if
with claws. INEZ. EMILY. NOAH. MICAH. MJ, KLB. IN (or HZ, depend-
ing on how you read it). Pick any two letters. There is a multiplication of equations: S + J, KD + MN. J + A 4 EVER. A + C = ♥. JOHN +
CHRIS. SHAILA Y MARTIN 2012 . . . Some of them so fresh, so viscous
green, they might have been excavated this afternoon.

In a certain light, this place is violent (and how the light does
shift as the clouds pass in a high wind, spotlights playing through
the trees). There is, here, the pseudomasochistic attempt to define
another's skin. Don't pretend you don't see it. These trees are nothing if not figurative. They have accidental pimples and impromptu
teats, swellings and cavities where the trees' flesh has died back
or grown over broken limbs. And I don't doubt that some of these
carvers imagined the skin of a madrone was someone else's. Or
their own. We play at vivisection, at surgery. We are the tattoo or the

tortured artists. This walk is a reminder that stories (you plus me) are often scouring, and sometimes involve the erasure of something. What is an essay, or a book, but an incision into a tree?

But most carve not because the tree stands for the body — not consciously, I believe — but because it is softer than rock. These madrones present themselves, a supple medium to bind our love in its blindness. There is such ultimate sweetness in such severe writing. This trail is a lovers' arbor, a linear bower with a long memory of holding hands. After all, the primary symbols here are pluses and hearts, one kept safe in the bubble of the other. And maybe it should come as no surprise that before the heart symbol — that dimpled inversion of a teardrop — came to mean "love" in the thirteenth century, the shape already existed on heraldry as a representation of foliage. Of water lily and ivy and, in nearby forests, the sorrel that lies at the feet of giants.

There are, as well, the stars and crosses of sanctioned faith, but the difference between a plus sign and a cross, I see now, is a mere and tenuous extension. *Jesus Team A* is also carved here and there, and is everywhere implied, I imagine, for those who carry the letter in their hearts. Nearby is the circle-A of anarchy, and, as I near the summit of the trail, another svelte bole reads, *Dios te quiero mucho* — *God I love you so much* — in a vertical cascade. But who is this *you*: God, or some other affection?

All of these symbols, these letters, are a kind of arrow pointing to the self as well as to the ancient plateau of Lower Table Rock, where you can stand on the edge of basalt cliffs and look out at the fertile Rogue Valley, a gouge in time. Where you can survey the S-curves of the river and the pear orchards, their white spoiling blossoms, and see Medford in the distance and Interstate 5 cutting

through. Mount McLoughlin is a snowy stratovolcano on the horizon. The red-faced vultures soar along the cliffs below, swerving
hard in the warm updrafts that blow across our cheeks.

The madrone, I should say, was given its name by a certain
Father Crespi on the first Spanish expedition into Alta, California,
not far from where I grew up beside San Francisco Bay. He didn't
care for its native name — the Spanish had come to evangelize —
and he didn't name it the refrigerator tree. Instead, this tree, which
from Baja to British Columbia grows along the coast wherever it
isn't too wet, made him remember the *madroño* of his homeland:
the strawberry tree, with fruits that do resemble *fresas*. It is another in the *Arbutus* genus, a close relative of our madroño. And
"the Strawberry Tree," you might be interested to hear, was also
the original name for Hieronymus Bosch's most famous triptych,
the altarpiece now in the Prado known as *The Garden of Earthly
Delights*. In the early sixteenth century, paintings weren't titled, but
in the catalog of the Court of Spain, this one from the Netherlands
later became known as *La Pintura del Madroño*.

The left panel of Bosch's wild masterpiece is the unblemished
paradise of Adam and Eve; the right depicts a wondrous but woe-
ful damnation in an underworld of fire and demons. The largest,
the center panel, overflows with a strange fantasy of nudes and
fruits, either a picture of sin before the flood or, perhaps, if we
read more generously, of paradise realized. No one really knows;
we interpret according to our tastes. Pale, attenuated bodies lean
against and pick from the strawberry trees; they hold and wear
what look like cherries but which, to my mind, could just as easily
be the edible berries of our madrone: bloodred and a favorite of
birds, but mostly tasteless to us. Bosch's people seem to cavort

and contort with each other and animals in a landscape of excess that if you study their small faces, isn't necessarily the same as bliss. Nor is it meant to be.

Here I stand, alive, in the garden *del Madroño*. There are nudes all around, twisting. There is love, and there are the knives that lacerate it. That prove it. Off the trail, in a nexus of trunks, I even find one on the ground: a burnished, winking serration with a black plastic handle. The knife lies dropped or hidden, as if a couple had been caught in the act and fled, leaving this evidence, as if they wanted it to be found. As if they planned to return and continue their clandestine, bawdy art. To cut their hearts out all over again. Or is it left here intentionally so that others—so that I—will take it up and add to the writing? I think of the third panel of Bosch's garden, a netherworld where knives loom, splitting a pair of gigantic ears and piercing hands and stomachs. Pinning its people like moths. This realm is hinged to all the others.

Soon I begin to doubt whether particular windows into the gray heartwood are old letters or natural scars. Soon the innate patterns of bark, all checkers and curls, begin to pulse and blend with alphabet. I think a tree says *fear*, when it may say *pearl*. I think a heart holds DAD, and am disappointed when it is only D + D. Everywhere on these trees is the reminder of growth and change. All these letters will be distorted, subsumed, by new skin. Even the deepest shapes, the largest hearts, slowly infold. Most of these equations are left unfinished. Gradually the living phloem moves forward, like a lava flow always on the verge of cooling.

The biggest trees hold the longest memory, but it is the younger madrones that are ripest for paring, with their soft, herbal skin. Those near the trail's few benches (also carved) are especially vulnerable, most popular, and I wander through these groves, a voyeur with his instruments—his camera and his notebook. RED-NECK, reads one tree, and the words are so apt, so freighted, they rise to utter significance. They're stacked one atop another, the hyphen a copy editor's afterthought, the words a put-down and a coming together and a declaration of identity. But I think also of all the necking that has gone on in places like this, from here to 4 EVER.

Down the trail comes a pair. She is, like the hue of the madrone, a redhead, and her shoulder-length hair is windswept like the meadow and its ephemeral pools atop Lower Table Rock; her eyebrows are pierced, a deflated backpack is on her shoulders. He is wearing black-and-white camo shorts that hang below his knees, tall white socks pulled over his angular calves. His black T-shirt reads FRIED CHICKEN AND GASOLINE, and I don't quite know its degree of irony. Down the trail they flow, holding hands, a jaunt in their step and with the relaxed, faint smiles of electric companionship. On this unexpectedly sunny afternoon, his exposed and chiseled triceps have burned rosy. Their necks are the pink of their affection. A hermit thrush sings from the understory with its ruddy tail.

JAMES THOMAS STEVENS

In the Defile

We wake so rarely together, and when we do
the leaves have already left horses for trees.
We didn't realize when
moving to the canyon, we'd
given up sunsets for good. Gold and
red for cottonwoods and clay.

Here, woodpeckers grouse in the piñon boughs
and your sun-brown hands gather the brownest shells.
We root about like curve-billed thrashers,
silent beneath our chosen trees, try not to speak
of the current news. Pitch-laden
needles pressed to sore knees and palms.

A flicker lands on a branch above,
and we look up but beyond, to
the other side of canyon where
leaf-bare horses sleek and resplendent
gallop through ochred grass.

And when your cupped hand pours
piñons into mine, the edge of your palm
angled to my own, there is relief in knowing.
I take it all down — documented.

LANCE GARLAND

Brothers in Arms

Legacies of trash and love aboard a Navy frigate

O N THE WEATHER decks of my naval warship, in the wilderness of the Pacific Ocean, I smoked alone. It was my second deployment, my first without Easy.

Very little signified time's passing, save for sunsets and cigarettes. Cigarettes like scratch marks on prison walls to count the days, scars on the walls of my lungs. We didn't get breaks for their own sake, but I found a loophole: the weather deck, where my new habit could buy a few minutes of rest.

In my smoking reverie, fellow sailors approached me with words of apprehension.

"They've started an investigation."

"They're monitoring your e-mail."

"Cover your ass."

"Tell everyone it's not true."

"You can't possibly win."

"You know what's coming."

Over the course of the first few weeks of our six-month deployment, faces from the 250-man crew would sift before me like a kaleidoscope of melancholy colors. Nauseated and dizzy from the

onslaught, I inhaled one cigarette after another, leaned against the
side irons, and trained my gaze on the gray sea. I couldn't possibly
know how to respond, but most of them weren't there to listen anyway. They were characters in a drama, all playing their roles.

A southern man and his two friends stared at me, like wolves
stalking a weak member of the herd, waiting to strike. They were
friends of the accused man, and as I averted my eyes from them
and looked toward the thrashing sea below the ship, I imagined
his threats against me coming to life. Perhaps one of them would
collide with me as I walked the long gangway down the exterior
of the ship. A dark figure would push me into the lifelines—the
retractable railings that were lowered for gun shoots—and shake
my body against them, whitecap waves roiling below me like
shark teeth.

"If someone were to fall out here," I was warned, "they wouldn't
be found."

I could hold on to few things during this period of my life,
amid the chaos of faces, information, and uncertainty, and those
things composed what truth I could cobble together at any given
point. The truth about myself, who I was, and what happened to
Easy. But one night, as I smoked and mused about feeling lost at
sea, a spectacle revealed itself in the waters before me. All around,
from every vantage point I could see, lights rose from the depths
of the ocean. These clusters of bioluminescence glowed with
neon green-and-blue sparks, rising from the deep as exploding
universes. Water radiated with those solar systems, galaxies of
glowing life. The cloudless sky reflected the phosphorescent emis-
sions as stars of the empyrean inverted from nebula-like clusters
rising from the sea. I sat between all splendors and felt the utter

insignificance of my existence, and somehow, this signal from the sea made me feel less alone.

About a year and a half before—on the day I was given an introductory tour of the USS *Rodney M. Davis* and my new job as gunner's mate—I crossed paths with a swaggering boatswain's mate who held the coveted bosun's pipe. He was a second-class petty officer, the second-in-command of my new ship's boatswain department, with a joker's smile and a few teeth capped in silver. The bosun's pipe was a whistle, but more so, a symbol of power, and with its trill he could command his crew of seaman to do his bidding. His nickname was Easy, short for Ezekiel.

On our first port of call, the shores of Okinawa, our eyes wouldn't stop meeting. We were soon inseparable, in large part because I'd taken up smoking. We'd light each other's cigarettes with our own, daring, when no one else was around, to keep them in our mouths the whole time, our heads leaned in, the tips kissing.

In the luxurious foyer of a four-star Singapore hotel, he told me he would reserve a room if I stood guard by the front door. I sat in the air-conditioned lounge, trying to dry the thick sweat from my body, and I watched Easy out of the corner of my eye. My nerves were like lightning. I had no idea what I would say if we were caught. I hadn't been granted overnight privileges, and we had to be back to the ship by 2000 hours. There was no reason why we would be spending $400 on a hotel room we'd only use for a few hours.

As Easy was finishing the paperwork, the only two female officers on our ship walked out of the elevator and turned their heads, seeming to recognize him. My legs went limp. The women then turned and headed straight toward me. With no other option,

I jumped out of the armchair and lunged for the nearest door. Once outside, I ran around the street and snuck back in through a side door. I found Easy by the elevators looking painfully exposed, and pulled him into an elevator.

Six hours in the bathtub together, smoking cigarettes, drinking whiskey, we forged the sex of starvation, physical passion that permeated the room with nicotine vapors. I was twenty years old.

Afterward we tried to wait for the safety of port visits, where we got better at finding hotels no one frequented, but these visits were few. One was in Brunei, a country that would soon grant the death penalty to those like us. We didn't bother with a hotel there, but we did find our way to a restaurant bathroom. The risk of that act would take years to comprehend.

Back on the frigate, we searched for locked spaces, dark corners. We tried the boatswain's locker at the very front of the ship, which had two watertight doors, each with eight dogs that had to be opened, one at a time. We were confident that no one could take us by surprise there. But our first time in that sweaty space, half-clothed, we heard the sound of a door being unlocked. As each dog clicked open, our stomachs sunk.

"What will we say?" I whispered, squeezing his sweaty forearm.

"I don't know," he whispered back, looking around frantically. He pointed to the angle irons—shelflike support beams that reinforced the hull of the boat and doubled as storage space for all kinds of greasy lines and levers used for mooring the boat. "Climb into the gear locker."

I zipped up my coveralls and climbed the bulkhead just as the first door opened. Easy pushed me upward as the second door began to click. We heard the first dog unlock, then the second.

I climbed onto the shelf—feeling the anchor-chain grease smear all over me—into the rigging and tackle, and pulled piles of heavy rope over me to hide. The loose fibers from the coarse rope stuck to my greased skin like feathers.

A third dog opened. I held my breath. There was an interminable silence, and then a footstep, two, and the sounds of the dogs shutting. The intruder had disappeared, closed the first door behind him. After an excruciating amount of time, I crawled out of the gear and slid out to the smoke deck while doing my best to shake off the fibers and wipe away grease. A few minutes later, Easy joined me out there, and we stared at the dark sea night, pretending nothing at all could possibly connect us.

This became our routine—close calls and forbidden sex—although we made sure to find better spaces that didn't threaten us with getting caught. We would meet in the dark of night, relieve each other of the stresses and silence the job required, then make our way, one at a time, out to the smoke deck for a midnight cigarette. Eventually I became the sole technician on the ship's gun mount—a two-story cannon with a vaultlike space secured from the inside by a hulking watertight door. Like Easy's bosun's pipe, I carried the gun mount's many keys on a lanyard that hung at my hip and jangled as I walked about the ship. That wonderful MK 75 would become our private apartment for the rest of our deployment.

Each of the four walls of the gun mount housed shelves that contained missile canisters stacked in rows twenty high. The revolving magazine—which resembled an enormous cylinder from a six-shooter revolver—was suspended in the center of the space, free-hanging, and housed eighty of the blue-tipped, ammunition rounds: it could empty these rounds in under a minute.

Higher still, up into the second story, was the barrel housing, where rounds were transferred and firing commenced.

Inside our second home, I set up a workingman's bookshelf from used ammo cans in a pile that rose to the overhead. The carefully arranged and lashed gunnery boxes held heaps of literature. I was deep into the transcendentalists: Emerson, Thoreau, Whitman. I found fellowship in a copy of *Leaves of Grass* from my father. A nurse during the Civil War, Whitman wrote poetry some considered scandalous; he could not be open about his sexuality. He wrote in *Drum-Taps*: "As I lay with my head in your lap Camerado . . . I confess I have urged you onward with me, / and still urge you, without the least idea what is our destination, / Or whether we shall be victorious, or utterly quell'd and defeated." Like Whitman, I was compelled to serve, to stand by my brothers in arms in wartime toward peace. And like Whitman's, my love for men was considered scandalous. While serving my country, I was legally bound to hide my sexuality.

Though I can't say that Easy and I were always discreet. One night the two of us fell asleep atop a yoga mat on the deck below the bookshelf. Like all the ship decks, it was made of nonskid material: hard and sharp to give traction to sailors walking in rough seas. But we'd found such comfort in each other that we slept well through that night, our only full night together, waking to the sound of the reveille bells. Fear flooded the space as we both clamored to dress ourselves. Easy quickly headed to the smoke deck, and I followed shortly thereafter.

A time or two, people seemed to notice that Easy and I would smoke at about the same time every night, but we always blew them off. We play video games together, we'd say, like a lot of other guys did at night. No one ever asked which ones. No one ever pointed out that I didn't even have a video game console in the gun mount.

But eventually I'd had enough of hiding, and on my social media page I decided to change my orientation to "gay." In so doing, I had transgressed the military's Don't Ask, Don't Tell policy. For that brief moment, I felt unanchored to other people's ideas about love, expansive and oceanic and free.

A lot back then was not asked and not told. Inside the lower level of the gun magazine were heaps of used ammunition canisters filled with trash. Once every few weeks, in the shadow of night, my supervisors would take us to the gun mount and line us up in a chain gang that extended down the hatchway ladder and out the starboard bulkhead door, each man within arm's reach of the other. From there, we'd throw our waste overboard and watch as the canisters floated at first, then slowly filled and sank into the dark waters.

We used pike tools to poke holes into metal ammunition canisters; any splash they made was muffled by the noise of the waves. Oily rags, solvents, chemicals, perhaps even used paint canisters. A wreckage of trash trailed behind us like flotsam from shipwrecks. I imagined the canisters never reaching the seafloor, but instead piling on underwater ridges of trash mountains from decades, perhaps centuries, of dumping—an unseen, underwater wasteland. Everything seemed so backward. Loving Easy was punishable by discharge, but throwing trash overboard was standard practice. I felt like the debris I threw out to the sea. Our supervisors called it night ops.

Night ops were a regular part of being on deployment, especially when a port visit was canceled and the ship began to overflow with trash. Our ship had a plastic waste compactor that turned the

myriad plastic refuse into giant disks, which were easily stowed
away. But what of the rest? What of my legacy on the waters I traveled? Like the trash, I felt disposable, easily discarded, and began
to see how our society floated on this concept of expendability. On
the smoke deck, my hands stained with chemicals, I marred my
lungs again and again with the markings of containment, hoping to
forget. At some point Easy would appear, his greasy forearm resting
on mine as he took the cigarette from my mouth, lit his with it, and
gently put it back between my lips. He'd leave his arm next to mine
as we leaned against the angle irons and looked beyond the ship
that stayed us. In resignation, I threw my used butts to the sea.

In the final months of that first deployment, I was hit on by
another sailor. Easy revealed that this man had molested him in his
sleep. He made me promise to never tell anyone. The sailor also
threatened my life if I spoke about it. But once we returned to our
homeport, the JAG lawyers called me in for questioning, and I told
them everything I knew. They said they'd heard similar stories and
were starting an official investigation. A court-martial began, and
with it came a series of inquiries into my relationship with Easy. As
gay men, we could not change our designation of dishonorable; we
were the military's refuse. Our new classification—and my broken
promise to Easy—pulled us apart.

I began my second deployment without him and with an investigation ongoing. The court-martial had not yet been scheduled,
but its certainty worried me constantly, like a dark storm visible on
the horizon. We sailed south, toward Central America, the Pacific
Ocean reflecting an incessant, scorching sun. I was often the only
sailor at the top of the ship, surrounded on all sides by a blinding

landscape of glimmering water and light. When I had first arrived, I enthusiastically climbed on top of the barrel of the gun mount and rode it like my grandfather rode broncos in Montana. Now the greatest effort I could command was leaning over the barrel as though over a fence that divided my life.

My future was in the hands of Commander Bradbury, a man I knew nothing about. Though the trial centered around Easy's abuser, my role as a witness was based on the credibility of my testimony, and this invited investigations into my character. I had now officially broken the law of Don't Ask, Don't Tell. My commanding officer was required by law to discharge me, and the decision of how to do so would be his alone. When I was summoned to appear, it was not at the CO's quarters, where business was normally conducted, but at the office of the command master chief, the highest-ranking enlisted man on the boat.

I arrived at the door, which was adorned with the golden knotwork of boatswain mates, and I knocked three times and stated my rank. I stepped into the room and saluted with the usual decorum. Master Chief shut the door behind me. The room shrunk to a point of vibrating suffocation.

"I think you know why you are here," the commanding officer said.

"Yes, sir."

"As long as I've had command here, I've heard of your outstanding reputation. You've never been in any kind of trouble, and you've grown to garner the respect of the crew."

He seemed to walk a winding cliff over the course of his monologue, and I followed his every word, trying to read into what the decision would ultimately be.

"But this impasse is not beneficial to our cause," he went on. "These recent developments have an obvious impact on the ship as a whole. I say this so that you understand the position you have placed us in."

Pinpricks of fear raced down my spine as I waited for him to finish his thought.

"With that said, we thought it appropriate to deal with this issue immediately and not drag it out through the deployment. In our eyes you have represented the Navy's core values with unswerving devotion. Even in the midst of hardship, you've upheld our core values of Honor, Courage, and Commitment."

I could not speak. There was a smile in his eyes as his face maintained its stoic facade.

"That concludes our meeting, Petty Officer," Master Chief said, extending his arm toward the door.

We stood, and I saluted the command master chief. He looked me directly in the eye, and an expression that reminded me of my mother passed across his gaze, as if I were his own, of the same blood. I did an about-face and headed for the door, but then I heard his voice behind me: "One more thing, Petty Officer . . ."

I turned back around and saw a look of authority once again on his face.

"No more 'friends.'"

I locked the gun mount's door behind me and collapsed to the floor in the same place that I'd held Easy that one long night. Thoreau's words from *Civil Disobedience* came to me from my bookshelf as I lay alone on that nonskid: "Unjust laws exist; shall we be content to obey them, or shall we endeavor to amend them, and obey them

until we have succeeded, or shall we transgress them at once." The
shame of my idealism, my insistence on truth, was the reason for
Easy's absence. It was the reason we were caught. But Easy was
violated, not only by the accused, but also by a law that stole his
identity, his love, and even his rights as a victim. I could not abide
the injustice. I had to act.

Later that night on the smoke deck, I held a cigarette in my left
hand and kept the open pack in my quivering right, ready to light
up the next in anxious succession. I'd survived that day, but a few
weeks later I would be flown from Panama for the court-martial.
Suddenly, instead of relishing the smoke that filled my lungs, I
began to choke. In the center of so many forces beyond my control,
I realized that smoking was one of the few things I could command. In that moment I didn't know that it would take me years to
quit the habit, and so many more beyond that for my lungs to heal.
Or that, like the scars on my lungs, oppression is written in the
body, so deep that it can be passed through our DNA.

The ship surged through the black waters, spreading great clouds
of chartreuse light and marking our path with the tail of a comet. The
bioluminescence offered me some solace, an understanding that my
CO had offered me a chance to heal, if I could see the years through.
The cigarette burned to the filter, leaving a long branch of ash in its
place. It singed my fingertips. I raised my hand to throw it overboard,
but stopped. I turned to the tin can I'd seldom used and tossed the
butt onto the small pile of ash. Closing the open pack in my right
hand, I lost myself to the marvel of lights below.

ELLEN BASS

Roses

Four roses drinking from a blue vase,
the first one I name Moment of Gladness,
the second, Wresting Beauty from Fear.
All year I watched my beloved disappearing, the sweet fat
of her hips, her laughter, her will,
as though a whelk had drilled through her shell,
sucked out the flesh. Death woke me each morning
with its bird impersonation. But now she has cut
these Clouds of Glory and a honeyed musk sublimes
from their petals, veined fine as an infant's eyelids,
and spiraling like any embryo—fish, snake, or human—
and she has carried them to me, saturated
in the colors they have not swallowed,
the blush and gold, the razzle-dazzle red, riven
from the dirt to cleave here briefly.
And now, as though to signify our fortune,
a tiny insect journeys across the kingdom
of one ivory petal and into the heart
of the blossom. O, Small Mercies sliced
from the root. I listen
as they sip the blue water.

ALEX CARR JOHNSON

How to Queer Ecology:
One Goose at a Time[1]

I ONCE THOUGHT I KNEW what nature writing was: the pretty, sublime stuff minus the parking lot. The mountain majesty and the soaring eagle and the ancient forest without the human footprint, the humans themselves, the mess.

Slowly, fortunately, that definition has fallen flat. Where is the line between what is Nature and what is Human? Do I spend equal time in the parking lot and the forest? Can I really say the parking lot is separate from the forest? What if I end up staying in the parking lot the whole time? What if it has been a long drive and I really have to pee?[2]

The problem is: the Nature/Human split is not a split. It is a dualism. It is false.[3]

---

[1] Before we sashay through this overgrown garden, let us set the proper footing.

I write these words from Dgheyey Kaq' on the shore of Tikahtnu, the unceded ancestral lands and waters of the Dena'ina people. In gratitude, let me honor the Dena'ina people and their generational stewardship of this home from time immemorial. Let me offer my thanks for the many thousands of years of good relations with this place and its inhabitants like the salmon and moose that still

1 (continued) feed us today. This home feeds my heart, just as it has for so many others before me. I offer my gratitude to those who know the names of the peaks to the east over which that spectacular full moon rises and upon which the long winter sunsets burn and melt and dissolve into nights.

The world has spun beneath your feet and mine many times since this essay first appeared in print nine years ago. To keep these words living for another year or ten, I've scratched out room for some offshoots, the hardiest of buds, the most succulent of chicks from the queerest of hens, if you will.

2 The line between human and nature grows messier with each passing day. We humans muddy the edges and mow over the meadows. There are more parking lots in more forests. More roads paved to the edge of more ocean shores. More contrails filling more blue skies. More blobs of warm bathwater bleaching more coral reefs. More men peeing. In the age of the Anthropocene, our footprints are precisely everywhere.

3 You already knew all this, though. Yes, yes, yes, you say to me. But what do we do about it? *There are problems, and they must be fixed!* Okay, well, if you are going to be that pushy, then the first step is for me to unsuccessfully resist rolling my eyes at your sense of entitlement.

That's a jerk thing to say, I know. It's hypocritical too, since the next thing I'm going to say is that the very first of all steps to solving any crisis is to do everything in your power to not be a jerk.

It's quite difficult for many of us, myself included, to avoid being entitled jerks. Not on our comment boards, not behind our desks or speakerphones, not in our Amazon carts, not from our ballot boxes, and especially not in our most elegant environmental prosodies.

Even so, it's a task and a responsibility, and one that we must each practice each and every day. How do we not be jerks? One way to start is to acknowledge peoples' existence. Not most people. Every person. Each one. What's more, acknowledge their humanity. Their right to exist. Their right to feel. To possess knowledge that you do not. To possess values that you do not. To practice religions you do not. To love in so many ways that you have not and cannot.

Even when given every opportunity to deny them, you must see them and honor them.

I propose messing it up. I propose queering Nature.[4]

.[4] Here's a perfect example of where, in the past, I was a jerk. When I "propose queering Nature," I am and always have been one of many voices in a kaleidoscopic chorus. The project of queering ecology draws from many fields of study and lines of thought, including queer rights activism, feminism, evolutionary biology, and liberatory social justice movements. I have always relied heavily on Catriona Sandilands's significant work creating space for queer ecologies. Joan Roughgarden and Timothy Morton's writings helped guide me at the beginning. Michel Foucault, Judith Butler, and more recently, Nicole Seymour.

Now that I've created space for more white people, it's time we center yet others who have long guided the rest of us even in the face of their erasure and silencing.

Here, see Kimberlé Crenshaw, who coined the term *intersectionality*. Hear bell hooks and Audre Lorde. Listen to Anna Julia Cooper and Sojourner Truth. Queer women of color have been leading the vanguard of a more liberated world more than I can possibly know.

See adrienne maree brown's recently published *Pleasure Activism*, which is electric, alive, and grounded in the embodied practices of generative somatics and Black Organizing for Leadership and Dignity circles.

"My body is a gorgeous miracle," adrienne maree brown says. "Don't let your body or your heart forget why we fight—to feel aliveness and togetherness. We will grow."

As it would happen, I'm queer.[5] What I mean is this:

---

[5] To be queer is to define your own otherness. It should not be surprising that those people who have been most erased, most othered—the oppression multiplied with each othering—may have the most practice, the most embodied history of making space for their own liberation, and in so doing, with or without their intent or consent, also lead the way for a conga line of liberation for all the rest of us.

See the beautiful trans queens and kings who set the conditions for the Stonewall uprising, who sparked the fire, and who wielded their power for the last fifty years even as they were continually erased from the record. See Marsha P. Johnson, who had hidden her queerness as a closeted young boy in New Jersey, but who made a name for herself as a performer and activist. Marsha was there at Stonewall when beautiful queer humans threw the first bricks and bottles.

Marsha was there with Stormé DeLarverie, famous in her youth as a gorgeous baritone drag king in the Jewel Box Revue at the Apollo Theater. Later in her life Stormé was a bodyguard at Stonewall and one of the first to be arrested the first night of the uprising. She had been hit on the head with a baton by one of the police officers. She was bleeding and her handcuffs were too tight. As she continued to fight for her life, she shouted to all the other queers watching.

"Why don't you guys do something?" she shouted.

Marsha and the others did something. They rose up and fought back against the violence against them. They demanded the right to exist. So began the modern gay rights movement.

Johnson, along with close friend Sylvia Rivera, created the Street Transvestite Action Revolutionaries (STAR). The two fought for justice the rest of their lives. Johnson's life was cut short when she was murdered on the night of July 6, 1992. The police ruled it a suicide and the murderer was never identified.

I am a man[6] attracted to men. Popular culture has told me that men who are attracted to men are unnatural.[7] So if my culture is right, then I am unnatural. But I don't feel unnatural at all. In fact, the love I share with another man is one of the most comfortable,

---

[6] I'm a cisgender man. I was a man born male. Thanks to what happens to be swinging between my legs, I walk through life safer and more easily. What's more, I can pass as straight when I need or want to. I can hide in plain sight from those who would like to hurt or kill me.

Those people still exist, those who have been transformed to hate me in their hearts. There are others, too, who wish to marginalize, erase, and deny my existence as a man who possesses the delightful physical capacity to love other men. Even so, my many other privileges help me live my life in comfort and relative ease. Where my oppressed queerness has closed doors, my cisgender white male status has opened so many others.

[7] Even with loving, supportive parents who did everything the best they knew how to do, I was exposed to the prejudices against queer people every day of my life. Gender was policed at every turn, in schools, churches, all public spaces. Religious leaders denied me queer role models and teachers. As a child, I watched as the federal government failed to protect queer people and people of color from the AIDS epidemic, over and again, year after year. Even at the height of the epidemic, queer bashing was all-too-frequently lighthearted entertainment on television and in film. A part of me died a little with every dumb homo joke, every fearmongering headline, every adult who distanced themselves from my existence.

honest, real feelings I have ever felt. And so I can't help but believe that Nature, and the corresponding definition of "natural," betray reality. [8] From my end of the rainbow, this thing we call Nature is in need of a good queering.

---

[8] To be queer is to live a truth we were told could not exist. To carry out the act of being queer is to create space for us—our lovers, our families, our friends, our *lives*—to exist. No matter how destructive it might feel for those who have benefited from the social structures so long and violently enforced, those structures were always artifice. At their most fundamental nature, those structures erased the existences of so many others. Those structures must be broken down and rebuilt if we are to fix anything.

To be queer is an essentially creative act.

Certain mornings, I wake, and my heart opens wide. On those mornings I believe the world is big enough for all of us. Today is one of those days. The world is big enough for all of us.

Imagine all the fabulous space between us. Imagine all the gorgeous space between Woman and Man, between People of Color and White People, between Poor and Wealthy, Immigrant and Nationalist. I hope you like to dance, because look at all that wide-open dance floor. Grab a partner or two or fifteen. Go conga-lining right through the door.

Okay, now here's the real kicker. Imagine all the great wide-open space between Self and Other. Can you fathom that space? Can you feel the muddiness? Can you lean out over the void expanding out in all directions infinitely? Don't worry. I'll catch you if you go dizzy. I won't let go.

Step #1: Let Go of Ecological Mandates.

Not so long ago, I read David Quammen's essay "The Miracle of the Geese." In the essay, Quammen says this: "wild geese, not angels, are the images of humanity's own highest self." By humanity, I can only assume that he means all humans, collectively, over all of time. "They show us the apogee of our own potential," Quammen says. "They live by the same principles that we, too often, only espouse. They embody liberty, grace, and devotion, combining those three contradictory virtues with a seamless elegance that leaves us shamed and inspired." Quammen seems to be on to something. Who could possibly be against liberty, grace, or devotion? But then he starts talking about sex. How geese are monogamous. How a male goose will in fact do better evolutionarily if he is loyal to his mate. "They need one another there, male and female, each its chosen mate, at all times," he says. "The evolutionary struggle, it turns out, is somewhat more complicated than a singles' bar." [9] I'm a little concerned about the evolutionary struggle thing, but I'm still tracking. Life sure is complicated. And then he says this: "I was glad to find an ecological mandate for permanent partnership among animals so estimable as *Branta canadensis*."

Boom. There it is. Geese are wild. Geese are pure. They aren't all mixed up with the problems of civilization and humanity. What we really need is to behave more like geese. If you are a male, then you must find a female. You must partner with that female, provide for that female, fertilize that female, and love that female for the rest of your life. If you are a female, well, you'll know what to do.

When I first read about Quammen's geese, I'd been out as bi-sexual for a year. It was around the second Bush election, and I was writing very serious letters to my conservative grandparents about my sexuality and politics. Now I know why his essay, so considerate, so passionate, so genteel, hit me in the gut. I was not natural.

Step #2: Stop Generalizing.

My instinct is to give Quammen the benefit of the doubt; it was the late '80s after all. [10] Regardless of his intentions though, Quammen's notion that Canada geese offer humans an ecological mandate not only reinforces a Nature-as-purity mythos (against which humans act), but at an even more basic level, his assumptions are simply inaccurate: plenty of geese aren't straight.

---

[9] We are taught to avoid the wide-open dance floor. We are taught to be shameful about all the ways we can *engage* with others in the world. Cishet* people in particular have a penchant for shaming any forms of nonmonogamous or nonmarital sex. It's easy to see that they largely all drink from the same font of shame and guilt that we were all told to swallow. As if you didn't know, those waters run deep.

Do you know what other waters run even deeper? The sweet and clear waters of liberated desire. My husband and I have been working hard to unlearn the worst lessons we have been taught. I am thankful for teachers like adrienne maree brown and Dan Savage, who tend to the waters from that spring and offer others guidance in how to quench our healthy bodily thirsts in ways that are free of shame.

* Cishet is the term for cisgendered heteronormative people, men born male attracted to women, and women born female attracted to men. The fact that this category of people didn't have a name until recently is itself a remarkable example of the privilege of those who benefit from its privileges.

In 1999, Bruce Bagemihl published *Biological Exuberance*, an impressive compendium of thousands of observed nonheteronormative sexual behaviors and gender nonconformity among animals. Besides giraffes and warthogs and hummingbirds, there's a section on geese. Researchers have observed that up to 12 percent of pairs were homosexual in populations of *Branta canadensis*. And it's not because of a lack of potential mates of the opposite gender. "In one case," says Bagemihl, "a male harassed a female who was part of a long-lasting lesbian pair and separated her from her companion, mating with her. However, the next year, she returned to her female partner and their pairbond resumed."

---

[10] I'm growing out of the instinct—or conditioning—to give cishet white men the benefit of the doubt. If anything, I'm learning to give them the least benefit of the doubt. They have been the ones continually centered, and therefore, have experienced the least of the messy edges where all the realness of living in this world happens. All other voices have been forced to occupy the margins.

Cishet white men must share the columns of the pages, the center of the screens, the stages and board rooms, the pulpits and the highways. They claimed even the deepest wildernesses as theirs. They named even the wildest of lands for themselves and set them aside as proof of their own manliness.

I'm tired of proving my manliness. I'm tired of other men proving theirs. I want to live in my manliness. I want to love my manliness. I want to free my manliness like it's a bird with wings and the whole living world is the sky. Manhood is not inherently about power, just as womanhood is not inherently about nurturing. Both are about a certain broad, if not boundless, capacity to live and love in this world. These capacities almost entirely overlap.

If you were somehow able to stand on the ground beneath our great human flocks as we flew overhead, you could barely be able to distinguish us one from another, except maybe a certain tone of our honks, a certain way we moved our wings, who led and who fell behind.

Red squirrels are seasonally bisexual, mounting same-sex part-ners and other-sex partners with equal fervor. Male boto dolphins penetrate each other's genital slits as well as blowholes. Primates exhibit all sorts of queer behavior. Observing queer behavior in nonhumans is as easy as a trip to the nearest primate house, or a careful observation of street cats, or deer nibbling on your shrubs, or mites on your skin.

The world itself, it turns out, is *so queer*.

Quammen assumed that geese are straight because it was easy to do. It was easy to assume I was straight, too; I did so for the first eighteen years of my life. But generalizing about the hab-its of both humans and the more-than-human living world not only denies that certain behavior already exists, it also limits the potential for that behavior to become more common, and more commonly accepted.

Step #3: Honk.

I don't mean to insist that there is an ecological mandate for be-ing gay. My interest in queering ecology lies in enabling humans to imagine an infinite number of possible Natures. [11] The living world exhibits monogamy. But it also exhibits orgies, gender transformation, and cloning. What, then, is natural? All of it. None of it. Instead of using the more-than-human world as jus-tification for or against certain behavior and characteristics, let's use the more-than-human world as a humbling indication of the capacity and diversity of all life on Earth.

So many of us humans are queer. Across all social, political, and physical boundaries, 2 to 10 percent of people take part in nonheteronormative behavior. [12] Beyond the scope of sexuality, humans are capable of any number of imaginable and unimaginable behaviors. That I do not eat bull testicles does not mean the behavior is any less human than my eating baby back ribs. Why then, if I cohabitate with another man, sharing the same bed, yes even having sex in that bed with that man, [13] am I somehow less human?

A goose is a goose is a goose. [14]

---

[11] Due to the sheer diversity of lived realities that we are attempting to study, discuss, and understand, queer ecological thinkers have been moving toward the increasing use of the plural: queer ecologies. Because I just can't help it, I have to say I like the ring of queercologies. Or, even more, what if we begin referring to the collective queercosphere? Now that's a world I want to live in.

[12] We have upward of 753 million beautiful queer people around the world. That's well over twice the population of the United States. This number very well may be underestimated due to historical and ongoing oppression and marginalization worldwide.

From an evolutionary biological perspective, a rate of 2 to 10 percent poses real questions as to the *functionality* of homosexual behavior, particularly exclusive homosexual behavior. It challenges the basic assumptions of Darwinian evolution, and that challenge has been used historically to sterilize and destroy us.

Oh, the irony if, in fact, human capacity for queerness does in fact provide some sort of evolutionary advantage to humanity. I, for one, would bet my life on it. We queers are not mistakes. We are not aberrations. We are not dead ends. We are no less than any other. We deserve no less than to claim our own beautiful humanity and every power and freedom of existence that comes along with it.

Step #4: Acknowledge the Irony.

In a review of Peter Matthiessen's book *The Birds of Heaven: Travels with Cranes*, Richard White indicts the "relentless and blinkered earnestness" of nature writing. White claims that because of its "reluctance to deal with paradox, irony, and history, much nature writing reinforces the worst tendencies of environmentalism." White points out that Matthiessen's unflinchingly sincere narrative baldly contradicts the circumstances: "The birds are immortal, timeless, and they transport us back into the deep evolutionary past," writes White. "But then Matthiessen gives us the details. He is sitting in a loud and clattering helicopter during this particular trip to the Eocene."

If you depict cranes as pure and ancient, with no place in this modern world, then you must ignore all those species that have done quite well in the rice paddies. Writing about nature means accepting that it will prove you wrong. And right. And render you

---

[13] Each body is undeniable in its messy realness, in its wisdom and desires. In its instincts and essential drive to find pleasure. We are still taught to hate and fear our own bodies. We are taught to hide our own beauty and pleasure. I have found so much joy in my life by unlearning shame and guilt and fear.

Consider butts, assholes, anuses. I'm sure many of you reading this are still ashamed and embarrassed by your own. I understand. We've been told they are the dirtiest, ugliest, most disgusting part of our bodies.

Well, I'm happy to tell you that we've been told wrong. They are soft yet wonderfully sensitive, fragile and yet remarkably rugged. They can provide immense amounts of pleasure. And best part of all? Each and every one of us has one.

[14] HONK!

generally confused. Nature is mysterious, and our part in the pageant is shrouded in mystery as well. This means contradiction and paradox and irony. It means that there will always be an exception. Nature has always humiliated the self-congratulatory scientist.

Let's stop congratulating ourselves. Instead, let's give a round of applause to the delicious complexity. Let us call this complexity *the queer*, and let us use it as a verb. Let us queer our ecology. Cranes can be ancient, but they can also be modern. Might their posterity extend past ours?

We've inherited a culture that takes its dualisms seriously. Nature, on the one hand, is the ideal, the pure, the holy. On the other hand, it is evil, dangerous, and dirty. The problem? There's no reconciliation. We accept both notions as separate but equal truths and then organize our world around them. Status quo hurrah! Irony be damned.

Take sexuality, for instance:

We have come to believe, over our Western cultural history, that heterosexual monogamy is the norm, the *natural*. People who call gays unnatural presume that Nature is pure, perfect, and predictable. Nature intended for a man and a woman to love each other, they say. Gays act against Nature. And yet: we rip open the earth. We dominate the landscape, compromising the integrity of the living world. We act as though civilization were something better, higher, more valuable than the natural world.

Our culture sets Nature as the highest bar for decorum, while simultaneously giving Nature our lowest standard of respect. Nature is at our disposal, not only for our physical consumption, but also for our social construction. We call geese beautiful and elegant and faithful until they are shitting all over the lawn and terrorizing young children. Then we poison their eggs. Or shoot them.

What I'm getting at is this: those who traditionally hold more power in society—be they men over women, whites over any other race, wealthy over poor, straight over queer—have made their own qualities standard, "natural," constructing a vision of the world wherein such qualities are the norm. And in so doing, they've made everyone else's qualities *perverse, against Nature, against God.* Even Nature—defined impossibly as the nonhuman—becomes unnatural when it does not fit the desired norm: *the gay geese must be affected by hormone pollution!*

A man who has sex with a man must identify himself by his perversion, by his difference. If straight is the identity of *I am*, then gay becomes *I am not.* Women are not men. Native people[15] are not white. Nature is not human.

Instead of talking about nonconformity, I want to talk about possibility and unnameably complex reality. What queer can offer is the identity of *I am also.* I am also human. I am also natural. I am also alive and dynamic and full of contradiction, paradox, irony. Queer knocks down the house of cards and throws them into the warm wind.[16]

---

[15] I've learned to refer to "peoples," rather than people. Indigeneity is as diverse and dynamic as this spectacularly diverse and dynamic planet on which we live.

Step #5: Don't Fear the Queer.

If theses were still in vogue, I would tell you my thesis is queer ecology. But as Zapatista leader Subcomandante Marcos told Pierluigi Sullo from the forest of southeast Mexico (and probably from a table in a house in a village in that forest),[17] "I sincerely believe that you are not searching for a solution, but rather for a discussion." He's right.

So what discussion am I looking for?

Well, first, one that is happening at all. I've met many kind people (aren't we all sometimes?) who are so afraid of being politically incorrect that they don't speak at all—well, at least not about race or gender or sex (this on top of the three taboos of religion, politics, and money). *How do I know how I should refer to Indians? Or blacks?*

---

[16] Queering, by necessity, fucks shit up. It must break the fibers in the fabric of our society, to then weave them back stronger with maybe a little more color in the pattern while we're at it.

When I first wrote this essay, I worked hard to not come off as an angry queer. *No need to alienate people, after all.*

I realize now that there is a right time to be angry. There is a right time to crystalize anger into action, to pick up a proverbial brick and throw it. There is a time and place when people have been oppressed for too long, when scores of people, generations of gorgeous queer people have been erased, denied, beaten, and killed. There is a time when your friends and elders have all passed away from a disease that could have been stopped and treated. There's a time when your heart can't take the news of another friend dying by their own hands or by others. In a world where we are told we don't belong, people find ways to remove us.

Now is the right time, here is the right place—as we are all fighting for our lives—to shout out to your friends: Hey! Why don't you do something?

Or gays? Or bums, for that matter? It's just all so complicated now.
Queer, then, remains a gesture of hands under the table. A wink.

In the recent past, conversationalists have at least had the
weather to fall back on. But the heat records of late with their
strange winds of change have whipped away[18] that golden ticket
of banality too. So people stop talking, at least about difference, or
flux, or complication, altogether. And the floor is left to those who

---

[17] There's reason for people to be angry when others are actively working to
erase them. Subcomandante Marcos was writing on behalf of Zapatista solidarity
from the Lacandon rainforest, the largest montane rainforest in North America.
It is the unceded ancestral homeland of the Lacandon Maya, and the generational
homeland of the agricultural communities who banded together to form
the Zapatistas.

The majority of the intact rainforest is contained within the Montes Azules
Biosphere Reserve, which the Zapatistas and the Lacandon Maya intend to
inhabit. The forest contains sacred and traditional sites, along with over five
hundred tree species, and significant percentages of all Mexican bird, mammal,
butterfly, and fish species.

The Zapatistas were tired of having their land rights stolen again and again
and rose up on January 1, 1994, on the day NAFTA was enacted. Their uprising lasted twelve days. The Mexican government killed an unknown number of
people. Hundreds lost their lives.

Herein lies the essential conflict: How do we create a world where people can
live their lives on the land that feeds them? How can that land continue to be
home for the fish and butterflies and five hundred tree species?

As a queer ecologist, I know what must not be done, what we cannot do. We
cannot deny anyone their humanity. So long as we continue to erase our humanity, we will continue to lose our ecology. The Lacandon Maya, Zapatistas, and
Subcomandante Marcos knew as much.

"The world we want is one where many worlds fit," the Zapatistas declared
from the refuge of the Lacandon rainforest.

are the loudest and quickest, and who never had any intention of complicating their conversation with anyone or anything that doesn't conform to their tidy but limited worldview. [19]

Step #6: Enjoy the Performance.

The problem with unnameably complex reality is that it's really hard to pin down and even harder to write about. Yet anyone who gives a damn about the ecological health of life on Earth knows that there's no time for dillydallying. [20]

---

[18] The climate crisis is here, and the time is now. I live in Alaska, one of the places on the planet changing most quickly. Seas that once froze are no longer freezing. Whole towns are being washed away by waves. The permafrost is melting. Real people in their real homes are worried about how they will feed their families when caribou have moved away and whitefish disappear. The warm wind is blowing off dark, wind-capped, angry seas.

[19] We have teachers who walk among us. We have storytellers who are sharing their wisdom with us if we are willing to listen.

Several years ago, my now husband and I met dear friends of ours in Moab. These friends were sisters who had responded to the fracking boom in the Upper Green River Valley of Wyoming with a heart-centered community art project. In the process of developing the project, they collaborated with Terry Tempest Williams. As it happened, Terry was in Moab at the same time as our reunion, so she invited us to meet her at Back of Beyond Books. Terry had just published her book *Finding Beauty in a Broken World*.

We sat on the floor in a circle and talked about what the world needed from us. Terry asked each of us a single question: *How do we transform our anger?*

In the late nineteenth century, a Danish scientist named Eugen Warming first used the term ecology to describe the study of interrelationships between living things. Henry Chandler Cowles, a doctoral candidate at the University of Chicago, brought ecology across the Atlantic with the 1899 publication of his treatise on the succession of plant life of the Indiana Dunes. Instead of static forests and static lakes and static prairies, Warming and Cowles recognized that these features of the physical world were in flux. As Cowles wrote in his introduction, "Ecology, therefore, is a study in dynamics."

Queer ecology, then, is the study of dynamics across all phenomena, all behavior, all possibility. It is the relation between past, present, and future.

Yes, we need to act. But we also must recognize that any action is also a performance, and possibly in drag. [21] Any writer who chooses the more-than-human world as subject must acknowledge both the complexity and paradox contained within the subject of nature, as well as the contradictions wrapped up within the writer's very self. Such writers will write about the parking lot and the invasive knapweed and the unseasonably warm weather and how they are undeniably mixed up in the complications. The poet James Broughton calls it "the mystery of the total self." Henry Chandler Cowles called it ecology. [22]

---

[20] Now will forever be the right time to throw the brick. Now will forever be the right time to release your anger into wise and compassionate action, and in so doing free yourself and so many others along with it. The drag queens on the first night of the Stonewall uprising did the cancan in the protest line. They danced and screamed and laughed and cried. And in the process, they created space in the world for themselves and all the others who would come cancanning along beside them.

It is the relation within the human and the natural and the god and the geese and the past, present, future, body-self-other. A queer ecology is a liberatory ecology. [23] It is the acknowledgment of the numberless relations between all things alive, once alive, and alive once again. No man can categorize those relations without lying. Categories offer us a way of organizing our world. They are tools. They are power.

Acknowledge the power. Acknowledge the lie. [24]

---

[21] I bought six-inch-heeled black stripper boots a few months ago. I was inspired by Pattie Gonia, a drag queen who began posting spectacular photos of herself in heels on top of mountains, prancing through the forest, surfing in breakers. She took her greatest desires, passions, and fears, put them in a backpack, and then went out into the refuge of the wild more-than-human world to live her best life. The trick, though, was that she brought us all along with her, anyone who wanted to go. Anyone who needed a queerer space to feel alive in the outdoors. Anyone who had also secretly dreamed of putting on eyeliner, lipstick, and a wig. Who wanted to dance it *out* and *in style*. She used her privilege as a white man to extend an art form pioneered by queer women of color in the sanctuaries they had found for generations before. Pattie Gonia is most certainly not the first to leap out into the wild places, but she has proven to be one of the most fabulous. She's gone viral. She's a star now. May we, all the others that follow, find the path to the summit that much easier. I can't wait to see the queens and kings as they gallivant along.

[22] I call the unnameably complex more-than-human world absolutely fabulous. No, just kidding. I call it the queercosphere.

[23] I expect this will be its whole field of study someday in the not-too-distant future.

[24] And please, if it strikes you, do it in heels.

Step #7: I'm Done with Steps.

Not so long ago, my father and I drove out of the city of Chicago going east on the Skyway.

On a map, the eastern boundary of the city is clean. It curls southeast along the shore of Lake Michigan, then cuts south at Indiana as straight as a longitudinal line. On the other side of the state line are Whiting, East Chicago, and Gary, towns that only gamblers and family members visit. Everybody else just lives there.

In reality, the eastern boundary of the city has no boundary at all. It continues its concrete, steel, and electrical-line unfurling along the southern shore of the great lake of Michigan. We were two white men, hurtling on four rubber wheels down the concrete Skyway, a corridor of semis and freight trains and transistors and faceless industrial complexes blinking out toward the lake.

I don't recall what my father and I were talking about. I do recall looking out the window onto the gray April sweep of the old glacial lakebed.

Then I saw the geese. More of them than I had ever imagined could gather. V after V after W after I after V. One after another, each flock waved several hundred feet above the ground. It was spring, and they all flew east along the metal and concrete corridor. They flew along the shore of the lake. [25]

---

[25] Here's the real miracle of the geese: that they exist at all on this wild planet hurtling through the expanse. What's even more to this miracle? We, humans, also exist. At the very same blinking moment. The most miraculous part of all? We possess the capacity to love the geese. To love them for their beauty

Less than half an hour later, we reached the Indiana Dunes. There were trees: oaks mostly. We opened our car doors to the calls of sandhill cranes. They were calls neither ancient nor modern. They were calls from the deepest present. As we stood in the parking lot, the car engine still pinging, the half dozen cranes swung across the opening above us and out of sight.

My father and I made eye contact,[26] then looked up from the parking lot into the trees where the cranes had gone. Then we both went off to pee.

---

[25] (continued) and their profligacy. Their cumbersome waddle and their graceful flight. Their honk and their bite. We can love them for their commitment and betrayal. Their spectrum of capacities in everything they do, from reproductive habits to companion rituals to whatever else they care to do with their wild lives. We can love them for how they continue to change. How they forever surprise us. We can even love them for how they frustrate and anger those of us who prefer poopless walks in the park. Because they can give us a chance to practice transforming our anger.

Form, function, and behavior. What does it take to love another living thing? Human, goose, dolphin, or duck. What does it take to see another living thing for what it is in its most essential state?

How do we learn to love?

[26] I once thought I knew what love was. It is so much messier, so much queerer, so much greater than I could have guessed. Love is greater than any single living heart could hold. I think that's why there are so many of us. Why there are so many others.

That is why each living heart is shaped so very differently.

JILL SISSON QUINN

Metamorphic

Notes on love, geology, and the limits of language

I AM ON ALL FOURS on the Lake Superior shore, ogling the contents of a pothole: pebbles and cobbles, water, and the sun's direct rays. Shirt sleeves rolled, I survey the colors—muted purples, greens, yellows, and blacks. I choose a stone, then reach in to retrieve it. So the process goes: like a god selecting souls, I compile a handful of stones, then move to the next pothole to see what it has to offer.

When we get home, my husband buys two field guides: *Is This an Agate?* and *Lake Superior Rocks & Minerals.* I've never been adept at identifying rocks. This granite we found—pink and speckled as a kestrel egg—is composed of quartz, mica, *and* feldspar. There is feldspar again in a pepper-colored rock I think might be diabase, but here the feldspar is mixed with augite and possibly hornblende, magnetite or olivine. You can see how things get complicated.

The difficulty goes deeper than simple composition. When identifying a rock, you often must detect the almost unfathomable process that melded its minerals together. Several of my rocks could be quartz *or* metamorphosed sandstone—quartz subjected to high temperatures and pressure, which would make them quartzite.

The only difference, my field guide says, is that quartzite has a little more texture. Identifying rocks, it seems, is more about parts than wholes, more about process than product. It is less about naming what you've found than about understanding how that thing came to be. In this case, how volcanoes, glaciers, and plate tectonics, over billions of years, produced and changed the rocks I hold in my hand. And how ten thousand years of wave action in Lake Superior smoothed them into something I want to take with me.

With flowers, categorizing is a simple matching game: look at the flower, look at the field guide picture. Is it the same size, shape, and color? Even birds, which can disappear in an instant, aren't as perplexing to me as the rocks I can carry home to study with the aid of a library of reference books. Once, at a relative's cabin in northern Wisconsin, an odd bird landed on the deck seemingly just to confound us. Warbler-size, the bird was a bright olive green with black wings and tail, blotches of white on its underside, and speckles and blotches of neon orange on its throat, head, and belly. It looked like a parakeet. But even without internet, and with only a few generic field guides dug out of a neighbor's basement, we identified it within three hours: a molting male scarlet tanager.

My understanding of rocks seems to go only as far as the broad divisions taught in grade school, and even on these categories I don't have a firm hold. So I look up definitions. Igneous rocks are basically cooled lava. Sedimentary rocks are compacted, cemented-together pieces of other broken-up rocks. And metamorphic rocks are rocks that have changed form. A University of Oregon website states: "Just as any person can be put into one of two main categories of human being, all rocks can be put into one of three fundamentally different types of rocks." Though the website clearly defines the rock types, it doesn't say anything about the two categories of human being, and I can't help thinking about the options that lie beyond the obvious divisions of male and female. Gay or straight? Accepted or marginalized? Convinced or uncertain?

I like to roam the forest naming things. Wood anemone. Rue anemone. *False* rue anemone. I wonder what makes the third one false: its more deeply lobed leaves, its slightly smaller flowers? It's a buttercup, like the other two, but not, my *Newcomb's Wildflower Guide* indicates, an anemone.

When I was an environmental educator, I taught a class called Stone Wall Study. I hiked my mostly elementary-aged students to a wall—one with its upper boulders spilled in the sun and gaps through which two could pass abreast—and asked them to speculate on the wall's original purpose, as well as to investigate the distinct habitats it now delineated. On one side was a red pine plantation; on the other, a mixed deciduous forest. *Which side of the wall looks more natural?* I would ask. *Did the wall keep something out or something in?* Once, during the class, I thought I had discovered a new species: on the wild side of the wall was what looked like an anemone with multiple tiers of petals, its flower a fancy petticoat, like some kind of double hybrid. When I couldn't find it in my books, I brought a local biology professor to check it out. Not a new species, he said, just an anemone with some kind of odd gene.

I don't know how well my students could imagine the farmer's sons who dutifully dug the rocks from the soil and piled them on the wall to provide safety for a few dairy cows, or the Civilian Conservation Corps crew that planted the red pines in the deserted pasture one hundred years later. Even with more life experience than my students, I myself have trouble imagining what I can't see, and what has occurred over a period of time longer than a life span. I am baffled by the process that created the rock, known as Shawangunk conglomerate, of which this particular wall was composed. I've always been plagued with a mental deficit for understanding composition, processes, and change—the kind of thinking the stones I have brought home from Lake Superior also demand—and this deficit has extended far beyond my ability to properly identify our planet's rocky foundations.

All my life I've battled a sort of dyslexia of cause and effect. On a recent canoe trip, I was mystified by a high browse line on the trees overhanging a lake. Did the deer stand in the water and dine? How tall could the deer possibly be? I wondered, until someone explained that in winter the lake froze, and they walked across the ice to graze. A weirder example: growing up in the early '80s, I lived for a while under the fear that contracting AIDS turned you gay. My older sister set me straight, telling me AIDS actually killed you. It didn't make you gay; gay people got it. I was, initially, relieved: if I contracted AIDS I wouldn't turn gay, only die. (Now, older and away from religious and family creeds, this response, of course, is embarrassing.) But almost immediately a seemingly darker worry surfaced: without a disease to cause homosexuality, how could I be sure to avoid this "affliction"? (For, at the time, that is what I had gathered from society that homosexuality was.) "How do you know if you're gay?" I asked my sister. The question arose from a presexual mind—one that couldn't yet fathom romantic love or physical attraction to anything. "You just wake up one morning and you know," was her response.

I couldn't understand how one day you would not know and the next you would, so I imagined it must be like getting your period—a milestone still many years off for me. I assumed you would open your eyes one morning and pull back the covers to reveal, on the bed sheets, written in blood, the universe's edict: gay or straight. I believed you had no say in the matter, that the issue was as tightly and long-ago cemented as a conglomerate's quartz and pebbles.

The issue, though, is much more complex. Some evidence does point to sexual orientation as something people awaken to—an inborn predisposition. Identical twins are more likely to both be homosexual than fraternal twins or non-twin siblings. And having several older biological brothers—whether you live with them or not—slightly increases a man's chance of being homosexual (from 3 percent to 5 percent), implying that the cause occurs prenatally. However, sexual orientation and sexual behavior are also considerably influenced by social and cultural factors. Among the Marind-anim people of southern Papua New Guinea, teen boys freely engage in homosexual relations with each other and with older married men, whereas all women are presumed heterosexual. In ancient Greece, men in their twenties permissibly wooed boys whose beards had yet to grow.

Perhaps my childhood fears were influenced by a society focused too much on sex and not enough on love. As it turns out, recent research and theory indicate that human sexuality—especially women's—may harbor a subtle plasticity. Whether you fall into the category of heterosexual or homosexual, your sexuality may include a secondary characteristic that enables you to fall in love with people who contradict your sexual orientation. Regardless of any "odd" genes or environmental conditions (in womb or world) that may lead to one or another sexual orientation, love, it appears, is ultimately metamorphic.

On the night of March 30, 1778, in Woodstock, Ireland, twenty-three-year-old Sarah Ponsonby donned men's clothing, grabbed a pistol and her little dog, Frisk, then climbed out the parlor window of the Georgian mansion where she lived with the family of her first cousin, Irish aristocrat William Fownes.

Twelve miles away, at Kilkenny Castle at ten p.m. that same night, thirty-nine-year-old Eleanor Butler, daughter of one of the period's most powerful Irish families, also put on men's clothing and secretly mounted a horse bound for Woodstock. Once there, she hid in a barn and waited for her dear friend. Avoiding unwanted marriages, they planned to travel twenty-three miles to Waterford, board a boat for England, and withdraw to the countryside to live together. Their escape did not succeed. The two women were returned to their families, who were relieved that the elopements did not involve men, which would have undermined the ladies' honor.

Sarah and Eleanor persisted, though, and openly now, in their desire to live together. Threatened with being sent to a convent, Eleanor escaped again, fled to the Ponsonby estate, snuck in through a hall window (aided by a housemaid), and hid in Sarah's closet. A day later she was discovered, but instead of coming to retrieve his daughter, Eleanor Butler's father sent word the two women could go away together. For ten days the Fownes family resisted, but when Sarah declared at all costs her one desire was "to live and die with Miss Butler," they too relented. Early on a May morning the two ladies left, with Sarah's housemaid, in a coach provided by the Butlers. Their journey ended in Llangollen, Wales, where they lived together for fifty years, studying literature and languages, writing letters and diaries, helping the poor, gardening, and running a small dairy. Despite keeping to themselves, they became widely known as "the ladies," and later "the Ladies of Llangollen."

For over a century, people have tried to identify what these two women *were*. Were they lesbians or, as we so diminutively tend to put it, were they just friends?

Attempting to identify my rocks, I pause at a page in the field guide between Jasper and Laumontite titled Junk. It is structured the same as every other page, with a map depicting junk's occurrence along Lake Superior in the upper right corner and the same headings, like HARDNESS and STREAK, in the left margin. Next to SIZE the text reads: "Beach junk can be as small as a shard of glass or as large as furniture or appliances." Next to WHERE TO LOOK the book says, "You can find beach junk all around the shores of Lake Superior." It's amusing to me that beach junk, though its name implies a lack of value, is important enough to have garnered a page in the guide and that, although the idea of beach junk having a universal hardness or streak is ludicrous, an attempt has been made to mold such a find into the accepted classification system of rocks and minerals. But I'm confused by the accompanying picture, which shows a porcelain tile, beach glass, rusty metal, an aluminum blob, slag glass, and a piece of driftwood. How does driftwood—something natural, something people collect—fit into the same category as discarded furniture and appliances—basically trash? I suppose it's all about perspective. Like being "just friends" when you might be lovers, to a rockhound, even driftwood is junk.

Most scholars call the eighteenth-century relationship enjoyed by the Ladies of Llangollen "romantic friendship"—a particularly intense, exclusive, intimate, asexual love between same-sex friends (either male or female) that may or may not include holding hands, cuddling, kissing, cohabitating, and sharing a bed. Though the term "romantic friendship" did not come into use until the nineteenth century, passionate nonerotic friendships had already existed and been considered ordinary for some time: Plato describes them in his *Symposium*, circa 385 BC; Montaigne describes them in his essay "Of Friendship," dated mid-sixteenth century. During Victorian times, romantic friendships flourished between middle- and upper-class women, likely because Victorian men and women—even married couples—resided in two opposing worlds, marriages were often arranged, divorce was rarely sanctioned, and women were assumed to be uninterested in sex. Thus, ardent female friendships—like the relationship between Eleanor Butler and Sarah Ponsonby—were tolerated and even encouraged.

These relationships have been tagged with all sorts of labels. Intimate friendships between college-aged women were termed "smashes" in nineteenth-century literature. "Boston marriage," another widely used phrase, originated in Henry James's novel *The Bostonians*. The phrase "mummy-baby friendships" comes from studies in Lesotho, South Africa, where intimate relationships between younger girls and slightly older girls are part of the female social order. Yet another name, "Tom-Dee relationships," is borrowed from Thailand; *Tom* is short for tomboy, and *Dee* for lady.

Even though contemporary America does have terms for intimate, nonsexual, same-sex relationships, such as "bromance" and "womance," it's hard for the modern American mind to understand and accept the concept. In the school where I teach, students titter at the way Brutus and Cassius speak of each other in *Julius Caesar*, throwing the words *love* and *lover* around shamelessly. According to Lillian Faderman, author of *Surpassing the Love of Men: Romantic Friendship and Love Between Women from the Renaissance to the Present*, society began scorning intimate same-sex friendships around 1920: "Such friendships are usually dismissed by attributing them to the facile sentimentality of other centuries, or by explaining them in neat terms such as 'lesbian,' meaning sexual proclivity. We have learned to deny such a depth of feeling toward anyone but a prospective or an actual mate."

As Faderman implies, everything today must be about sex. The idea of romantic friendship washes up on the shores of our post-Freudian era like so much beach junk, its field marks smoothed through the last century into something difficult to identify but simple to lump into a single, discriminatory category: latent homosexuality.

The Lord's Prayer of metamorphism goes like this: *limestone to marble, sandstone to quartzite, shale to slate, granite to gneiss.* I can recite it as if I am practicing for some kind of religious confirmation. But even as I utter the words, I don't really understand them. I remember the rock cycle. Igneous rock can become sedimentary or metamorphic. Sedimentary rock can become igneous or metamorphic. Metamorphic rock can become igneous, sedimentary, or even a new kind of metamorphic. But I am baffled by any description of how these processes actually work.

Limestone to marble, sandstone to quartzite, shale to slate, granite to gneiss. I recite the words again. At what point does the granite become gneiss? On what day? At what hour? That old dyslexia kicks in. Where is the line or the moment in time that divides what it once was and what it now is? Metamorphism, my source says, is impossible to observe; it can only be studied after some sort of weathering, erosion, or uplift. Often the processes that caused the change are tricky to discern. And metamorphism is not sudden; it takes millions of years for rocks to change.

The changes that we suffer within ourselves can be just as incomprehensible. For a heterosexual, falling into a particularly intimate friendship with someone of the same sex (or, for a homosexual, someone of the opposite sex) can lead to a small crisis of identity when considered within the restrictive categories we currently use to describe relationships and sexuality. When Basil Hallward first saw Dorian in Oscar Wilde's *The Picture of Dorian Gray*, he stated, "I knew that I had come face to face with some one whose mere personality was so fascinating that, if I allowed it to do so, it would absorb my whole nature, my whole soul, my very art itself." I have met a woman like this.

She is where I have never been. She is almost always where I have never been. This time it is Biakpa, Ghana. Her husband is ill, in bed. She reads and looks for insects. She feeds grains of rice to three types of ant colonies, watches snails mate, finds a cigar-size millipede. There are moths whose wings look like animal eyes or dead leaves, a green bug that looks like a green leaf, huge spiders, a caterpillar that hangs upside down from the ceiling with a tube that covers its body. Hard-skinned grubs stick to both the ceiling and the cement wall; their colors match what attracts them. She and the

local kitty hunt in the evening. Where she crouches and looks, it
crouches and looks, then it kills what she sees.

I know this because she has written me. In fact, what I have
written above is almost entirely plagiarized—her version of herself,
which she meant for only me to see. What I remember is her
turning to laugh as she locked the cabin door before a hike during
a three-day weekend in the woods, no husbands, in Michigan's Upper Peninsula. I was startled because I saw age in her face. The last
time I had felt so close to a friend I was young. And this woman
was as old as my mother was then, and I am old enough to be my
mother then, and neither of us are mothers—which is beside
the point, but maybe it isn't. Inside us are half of each child we've
never had and some small piece of all the women we've descended
from. When I admire the distal edges of her fingernails, white and
perfectly curved like the horizon of Ely, Minnesota, must have been
the weekend she went mushing—which I read about on her travel
blog (also there: a picture of her juggling with dried mud for some
children along the Mekong River)—when I admire these things, it
is because I love her passion for living.

One night, we are actually in the same place: full of seafood
and wine, seated between our husbands at the musical *Wicked*.
When the lovely Glinda, who becomes the Good Witch, sings to the
emerald green Elphaba, future Wicked Witch of the West, "Because
I knew you, I've been changed for good," she whispers, "That's us!"
and grabs my hand. I am taken by surprise. I whisper back, joking,
"I guess I'm Elphaba." I say this because my friend is beautiful:
hair the almost-black of the basalt I brought home from the lake,
eyes as blue as the kind of cloudless sky that almost everywhere,
you must patiently await.

For one week, in the month of July, I go to where she is. To her favorite place on earth: high desert, a place that's made of circumstantial evidence — dry riverbeds, already eroded buttes and mesas, a beauty mute and built on abstinence. She plans a ten-mile loop hike at Capitol Reef National Park, which sounds marine but water is scarce here. We don't have four-wheel drive so we have to hike five extra miles, round trip, to and from the trailhead. My husband comes along. Her husband stays back — at the end of our hike, he will meet us on the road, the blue plastic tub they use to wash their camp dishes filled with ice and a two-liter Diet Coke.

None of the dreams I had of hiking side by side, steeped in conversation, pan out because I hike much faster than she, especially on the uphills, which once or twice have made her faint. We hike to the lip of the Waterpocket Fold, a hundred-mile-long gash in the earth's crust, the rocks on one side lifted seven thousand feet higher than the other. It is dry, beautiful, alien. But by the end of the fifteen miles, I trail behind her and my husband, in so much pain I am crying. *It's because of the pounding,* she says. *These are not the soft soil trails of the forest. Everything is rock.*

She is where I would like to be. I do not mean that she is there. I mean that she *is* this thing: a sun-warmed rock next to a rushing stream — a rejuvenating combination of sunlight, stone, and water. When I travel, I seek out these things. Likewise, she is where my mind goes when it decides to wander.

Constant thought about the object of desire is a common sign of romantic love, as are a need for proximity and physical contact, despair at separation, elation when the object of desire gives you attention, and a tremendous awareness and understanding of the partner's moods. But in the article "What Does Sexual Orientation Orient?" Lisa Diamond points out that these feelings and behaviors also characterize the infant-caregiver bond. And who has not heard a new mother comment that she is totally "in love" with her child? Although we may not remember it, we were in love with our parents, too, during the first year or so of our lives.

The mistake most of us make is to assume romantic love evolved to ensure that mammalian mothers and fathers stuck together to raise their highly dependent young and, thus, that it occurs *in concert* with sexual desire, and is only legitimate when directed toward the opposite sex. But it's likely that romantic love between adults is what's known as an exaptation, a trait evolved for one reason but co-opted for something else. Here's why: from an evolutionary standpoint, long before there was "mating for life" there was the necessity for a mother to bond with her child—creating a totally physical, totally loving, but totally asexual relationship between her and either a daughter or son. The point here, as Lisa Diamond puts it, is that "romantic love and sexual desire are functionally independent," and "love knows no gender." In fact, humans may be biologically predisposed to experience romantic friendship.

The University of Oregon website that divided humanity into two undeniable (but unstated) groups gave this definition for metamorphism: rocks that have "moved into an environment in which the minerals which make up the rock become unstable and out of equilibrium with the new environmental conditions." So metamorphism is situation-dependent. It's the process of adjusting to some kind of change, usually caused by increased temperature or pressure. Above 200 degrees Celsius (392 degrees Fahrenheit) rocks begin to recrystallize. Whatever elements are available in the original rock will be broken down and recombined in a different way, creating new minerals.

If temperatures reach 600 degrees Celsius, a complete meltdown occurs: rocks become magma, which, when it cools, creates igneous rocks, something entirely new. But during metamorphism, nothing is lost or added at the elemental level. The basic composition stays the same, which is what is so complex about it: that the rock can still be what it is and yet be in the process of becoming something slightly different. What I don't get about metamorphism, that the metamorphism takes place while the rocks are in a solid state, is also perhaps what is so groundbreaking about new theories on human sexuality: according to Lisa Diamond, it is possible for a person's sexual desire to change in the context of a single relationship while that person's sexual orientation remains the same.

Diamond has coined the phrase "sexual fluidity" to describe this phenomenon. In her book by that name, Diamond addresses how most people believe that the biological order of a romantic relationship entails sexual desire first (that initial "chemistry") and romantic love (the intimate bond) second. But, Diamond's research shows, the opposite can also be true, especially for women. What begins as an intimate friendship can turn sexual. Different from bi-sexuality, which involves regular attraction to both sexes, sexual fluidity might happen only once in a lifetime, or only a few times, or not at all. The likely catalyst is oxytocin, a hormone that facilitates not only bonding between infants and caregivers (or close friends), but also sexual arousability. Simply hanging out with someone for whom you care deeply can—sometimes and for some women—

produce desires that conflict with a person's primary sexual orientation. In other words, the body's chemistry can temporarily change its own seemingly fixed tendencies. When this happens, the world may call you something different. But you are still you.

If you search Elizabeth Mavor's biography of the Ladies of Llangollen, or the diaries of the ladies themselves, you won't find a single hint of anything sexual. And neither will you here. All I can say is this: there is no field guide for love, or friendship, or the great variety of people one will encounter in a lifetime. And: this is not a coming out piece. It is about going inward.

One Christmas, we go with our husbands to Les Eyzies-de-Tayac, France. I want to see the engravings of early man, something inconceivably old. I arrange a visit to the Grotte de Bara-Bahau—an onomatopoeic name, given for the sound the large rocks that have fallen inside the cave must have made. We listen to a woman give a brief tour to just the four of us, in broken English. We strain to see in the rock the living things she traces with her laser pointer: a reindeer, a horse without legs and a horse without a head, and aurochs—an early ancestor of cattle. The bear is a bit easier: natural convexities in the cave wall itself form its head and shoulders, a large flint pebble acts as eye, and from its mouth is etched a long line, representing the animal's breath. Easier still is the phallus, which my friend points out privately to her husband before the guide even gets to it, not sure if it is an actual engraving or an instance of pareidolia—the imagined perception of a pattern or meaning where it does not actually exist, like seeing a picture in the clouds. "Oh, yes," the guide chimes in, overhearing. "There is a phallus." This is rather rare; more common are depictions of female genitalia, I later read.

We leave the cave, joking like teenagers about my friend's single-handed ability to identify the phallus in a cave of otherwise obscure engravings, but also about the strange question our guide repeated over and over during the tour, singling out each one of us, multiple times, as its recipient. "Do you *know*?" she would ask, the intonation and pronunciation of her mother tongue adding mystique to her inquiry. Then she would turn to the next one of us, making direct eye contact: "Do you *know*?"

"I do not know," she would respond to her own question. She seemed to want to preserve, in addition to the engravings, some other element of the cave's mystery.

On the shore of Lake Superior, among those wave-carved potholes filled with stones, I looked in, chose the ones I liked, and held them close. But just as the page on beach junk in my field guide suggested, I also found something in one of those potholes that I didn't expect. When my husband accidentally dropped a coveted quartz pebble into the largest and deepest of the holes, I rolled up my shirt sleeve as far as it would go and leaned over to recover the stone. Suddenly, I saw myself.

It must have been similar to what Narcissus experienced in that silvery-surfaced forest pond. Never before had I seen a clearer picture than what I saw that day in the pothole. I couldn't move. Like Narcissus, all I could do was gaze. Perhaps what kept Narcissus at the pool, in admiration over what was before him, was not self-love but a fascination with the image of himself as reflected by the earth. What I saw in that pothole, now a portal, was not made of skin and bone — the usual "junk" — brown hair, brown eyes, small ears, my father's nose. I was made of water and stone. Though we may label ourselves heterosexual, bisexual, homosexual, lovers, or just friends, we should not be surprised to find that we are as dynamic as the earth that holds us up. We are simultaneously solid and fluid, inherently uncategorizable. We are always in the process of transformation.

Originally, life on Earth was divided into two kingdoms: plants and animals. Then there were three; then four; then five; now six. Perhaps two categories — whatever they may be — are not sufficient for humans either. Names that come from without are destined to be inaccurate. It is not what we are called that we must answer to, but what calls us from within.

Joseph O. Legaspi

The Tree Sparrows

We suffer through blinding equatorial heat,
refusing to unfold the suspended bamboo shade
nested by a pair of hardworking, cheerless sparrows.
We've watched them fly in-and-out of their double
entryways, dried grass, twigs clamped in their beaks.
They skip, nestle in their woodsy tunnel punctured
with light, we presume, not total darkness, their eggs
aglow like lunar orbs. What is a home? How easily
it can be destroyed: the untying of traditional ropes,
pull, the scroll-unraveling. For want of a sweltering
living room to be thrown into relief by shadow.

The sunning couple perch open-winged, tube lofty
as in Aristophanes' city of birds, home made sturdy
by creature logic and faith that it will all remain afloat.

MARK SULLIVAN

My Love Feeds the Crows

In the park where I run,
I see people feeding animals
almost every day.
You've seen them too; usually
they're alone, often old,
sometimes disheveled, the kind
you think might not have had enough
friends in second grade.
They whistle for squirrels, lob
each one a peanut as though
perfecting their aim.
They seed the pavement
for pigeons, grains sputtering
over the surface like spices
hitting a hot pan.
At times they cast themselves
into statues so the birds
will flock to their fingers.
It's all about intimacy,

I've decided, letting
the species barrier fall
for a moment to see how much
will pass through. You know the feeling
of being caught in a thunder
shower, so drenched your clothes —
as if reversible — become
part of the storm? Not,
necessarily, an experience
you'd want, though some people
might. My wife has a weakness
for stray things, dogs dumped
in the park, wounded birds,
mice left to die on
glue traps. She leaves tins
for homeless cats, heaps
anthills of millet on
a stone wall for the sparrows
when she walks our dog. She'll even
feed the crows in bad winter
weather, scraps of fat and
sinew the butcher lets her have.
Sometimes when I take
the dog to the park, birds will
mob us for handouts, though I've hardly
ever fed them. They know
the dog. I can't quite describe
what it's like to find yourself
in the middle of this

swarm of flight and hunger,
tiny birds buzzing your head
like electric clippers. Like being
in an accident, jolted back
inside your body by the outside's
sudden insistence. Or as when
words fail and you can only
grope for sounds — that sense
of the inner and outer
pushed uncomfortably close.
And when you're in love
there's sometimes a dizzy pain
like blood rushing back into numb
skin, an odd sensation
of the truest part of yourself
walking out the door
without you. Maybe going
to throw strips of meat
to scavenging birds — something
you'd never do — and to listen
to the calls they make to
each other, how they fall
somewhere midway between
an echo and an answer.

CATE LYCURGUS

Bring You Apples

W E CLIMBED the gray-slatted lookout tower as the Lab bounded ahead, up stairs four at a time. Especially in autumn, after hiking the oak and beech woods of southern Indiana, my partner and I would stop for the color and sit in the window's ledge to gaze at russet leaking south.

I pulled two Pink Ladies from my bag and handed one to J. We sat quietly; only the sunk-tooth-rip chorus of bites punctured the fall air. Finishing my last mouthful, I noticed J held his own core between thumb and forefinger. *You ate the whole thing,* he said. And I had; I never wanted to bother with apple-trash and so plowed straight through the center, seeds and stem be damned. I nodded, took his from his hands, and swallowed its two woody bites. He kissed me. I don't know how many Wednesdays went this way, walking the rolling Midwest hills, but always, someone brought apples.

Rome, Gala, Golden Delicious, Fuji, Jonagold, Granny Smith, Opal, Envy, Arkansas Black, Honeycrisp, Winesap, Braeburn, or Jazz — my California go-to now, with J nowhere close. Still, come October, I'm back to apple-ing: cutting each to half-moon, quarter, chomping the square core. Peeling orbs in one long stripe, marveling at each watercolor wash, each lopsided flush.

J ate apples year-round, but I save up for their season. With seasonal eating, it's not yet, more not yet, then: apples on apples on apples. I start my recipe machine, inventing ways to turn pecks into months of dishes. I've served apples with stoneground mustard in a cheddar grilled cheese; spooned in warm maple compote over a stack of fresh crepes; stewed with steel-cut oats and walnuts; ribboned through French onion soup; shredded in radish-apple slaw; matchsticked with kohlrabi. I've had apples tossed with fennel and kale; stuffed with wild rice and baked; crisped; pied; sliced, peanut buttered; diced in dense cream cheese Bundts; halved-fat ways to starry rounds; splayed on pizza; crisped into chips; roasted with parsnips for velvety soup. You name it, I've tried it, I've made it: ways to savor apples for every meal of fall.

It's no wonder this has led to some hubris, to the belief that I can always improve upon what I'm given. I'm not alone here: think digging canals and erecting levees, managing deer populations, engineering Styrofoam cups. Apple growers go to great lengths for higher yields or shelf life, perfect crunch or optimal sugars. They devote millions to fight scab, rot, mealy flesh, bruising skin. It can take a solo orchardist a lifetime to cultivate a grove of sturdy hybrids, predict ripening, and anticipate frost or fire blight, given humidity. Rarely can she enact her will; rather, she must observe and react. Act as an usher when bounty comes, but concede some disappointments.

Malus pumila, with nearly twice the number of genes as me, and a multimillennial record of adapting, improving, and inventing behind it, has developed a reputation for sustaining and teaching us. What's more nourishing or wholesome: something to keep us

from doctors, to give to our teachers? Even Apple named its first
computers, portals to new worlds of information, "Macintoshes."
I'll often cut into an apple to find hypocotyls winding from its
center like tiny springs, ready to jet the seed through into the dirt; it
has all the sugar it needs. The future apple tree knows this package
(cotyledon, seed coat, fruit) is the smartest way to start. It trusts the
earth to provide.

As a girl, I recall thinking that if I ate enough, I could grow
apples from my gut. The myth of apples continued past girlhood to
a song the first boy I loved played me. In "New Year's Eve," Golden
Birds sings:

> And now I'm gonna bring her apples
> When she's in need
> After I suck the cyanide from the seeds . . .

> I'll have extra air for you
> Any time you start to drown . . .
> I'll bring you apples when your throat is sore.

In my last five years at home, I've tried to provide more than
apples, and, consequently, have ruined lots of dishes. Slices fanned
out atop the custard had lemon juice on them to prevent browning,
but it prevented eating, too. Hasselbacked fruit charred like slumped
armadillos, which I pitched straight from sheet pan to yard. In trying
to be ever more creative, generative, or useful, sometimes I've worn
myself out: live-in caretaking for my father can't keep the doctor
away. Teaching college résumé workshops can't germinate roots for
our Dreamers. Even fruit pies, J's favorite, I could never ship.

The other day, in the third or fourth bite of a miso-caramel-apple
pie, which she granted was delicious, my mamma said she was
really craving just a plain old apple. And I paused, sort of startled.
Bent down, and from the drawer pulled out one for her, one for me.
Even the bruised, lumpy orb offered crisp flesh, a star of seeds.
I swallowed a few in my surprise at just how cold, just how sweet—
at knowing we can take a little poison, that it comes with what also
might heal.

CYNTHIA HUNTINGTON

At Clapps' Pond, October

Three geese float on the shallow water, heads together inclined. They float at a distance, across the shallow water, among weeds and lilies. At the bend of the water where the land juts out, a shape that might be a heron. Its stillness solidifies and gathers shadow, weight of definition. We wait: it is a log. The geese are not moving except as the water carries them almost imperceptibly away from and toward one another, like a hand opening and closing. They float unaware of us. Low sun lights the treetops gold; soon it will fall into the trees and the leaves will fold it into their shade. We stand on the shore of the shallow, far-reaching pond, where boys fish for pickerel and bass. A fish jumps; a frog *unks*; the charge reverberates in memory; the past opens and we walk into it and know again in all our senses the sadness that could not be borne. And the peace under all that sadness. It says the world remains through loss, intact in grief. We stand on the shore where time folds, and we walk

with the dead and the living through many lives. And
you take me in your arms and pull me into you. I slide
my hands inside your jacket's warmth, and with our
kisses the geese waken, angry; they did not believe we
were substantial, our silence lulled them, they are
betrayed. Now they squawk and fly up, crying, to
denounce us. Their wings beat the air and are gone.
Furious spirits. I kiss you and kiss you, soften into your
shoulders; already this is memory; the past never ends,
we drink it together and pass into air, and still the
world remains. The sun nests in the trees now, settling
its wings. How soft the woods closing around us, the
swift cool after the sunlight goes, and the scent of
pine needles and dank water, clean air, a cloud of
gnats dancing in a slant of light. How alone we are
here, how the world seems to love us too.

GRETCHEN LEGLER

Gooseberry Marsh

THIS FALL on Gooseberry Marsh the weather is warm and the water is high. As Craig and I load the canoe on the grassy shore of the marsh, the sky is turning from rosy-gold to gray-blue. The blackbirds that make their homes in the reeds are singing by the hundreds, a loud, high, rocks-in-a-bucket screeching. Above us, lines of geese cross the lightening sky.

This is the first fall of our not living with each other, of living apart: Craig in the big house, me in a small apartment. But we decided to hunt together anyway, hanging onto this sure thing, hunting at Gooseberry Marsh, this thing we have shared for so many years.

We try in a polite and partly exhausted way to pretend that nothing is different, that we still love each other, but something subtle has shifted beneath us. It is more than the awkward and uneasy rearranging of our lives. In preparing for this trip, I bought *our* supplies with *my* money and brought the food to *Craig's* house. When we get *home* from hunting I will unpack *our* decoys and *our* coolers full of wet birds, do *my* laundry, and then I will leave for *my* apartment. We both feel embarrassed and sad when we catch ourselves saying, "Next time we should wear waders," for we both know there probably will be no next time.

But something more has changed. It is hard for me now even to reach out to hold his hand. The intimacy we had, the warm space between our bodies, has stretched so that it feels like nothing. Between us now is only this coolness, as we stand so close together on the shore of the marsh.

Even with the high water this year, we have to pull our canoe through the faint, watery channel between the forest of reeds that separates the two parts of the marsh. We both lean forward, grasp bunches of reeds in our fists, and on three we pull.

"One, two, three, pull," I call. "One, two, three, pull." We inch along. This is maddening. I can't steer the bow. Because Craig is pulling so hard in the stern and not watching, the canoe gets jammed nose first in the reeds. We have to back out and start over. I twist around in my seat in the bow and glare at Craig.

"Don't pull unless I say so," I say.

"Just shut up and do it," he says, wearily, coldly. "This isn't a big deal."

A sourness rises up in me. The nape of my neck bristles. He has never said anything like this to me. Ever. He has hardly raised his voice to me in seven years, not even in the midst of my most dangerous rages. I am so startled I fall silent. As we move out of the reeds into the pond again, I say quietly, "You were a jerk. You should apologize."

"Okay," he says mockingly. "I'm sorry I hurt your feelings."

On the far end of the pond we see frightened mallards and teal rise up, quacking. We know they will come back later. The sky around us now is a faint pink. The day is fast coming on. We open the green canvas packs in the middle of the canoe and one by one unravel the lead weights and string from around the necks of our

plastic mallards and our plastic bluebills, placing the decoys carefully in a configuration we think will draw ducks close enough to
shoot—one long line to the right of the place where we will hide in
the reeds, a bunch to the left, and sets of three and four scattered
about. I reach into the pocket of my canvas hunting jacket to feel
the hard, cold wood of my duck call. It has always been my job to
do the calling.

After our decoys are set and we have driven the canoe into the
reeds, pulled reeds down over us, stretched a camouflage tarp over
us, we wait. We hear sharp echoes from hunters shooting far off on
other ponds. The first ducks to come to us are teal. They are small
and tan, only as big as a grown man's fist. They land on the water
and we can see by the tinge of powdery blue on their wings that
they are blue-winged teal. We have set some ethical guidelines to
stick to, as we have every year. We will shoot no hens, and no birds
sitting on the water. We don't shoot the teal on the water, but I rise
up to scare them into flight so that we can take a shot. We miss.

The next birds are mallards and we shoot a hen. She falls into
the water and flaps around, dipping her head in and out of the water, slapping her wings. Then she sits up, confused and frightened,
and paddles toward the reeds. We know that if she gets into the
reeds, we will never find her again, that she will go in there and die,
probably be eaten by a fox or a weasel, or, eventually, by the marsh
itself. But I will still see our shooting her as a waste. My heart
cramps up as we follow this bird in our canoe, paddling fast, trying
to mark where she entered the reeds. We look for her for nearly
an hour, straining our eyes for curls of soft breast feathers on the
water among the reed stems. I engage in this search with a kind of
desperation. But she is gone.

"If it's still alive, it'll come out," Craig says. He is impatient to get back to our blind. While we have been looking, another flock flew over and flared off, seeing us plainly in the water.

I feel defeated and sad. We paddle back to our spot in the reeds, drive our canoe into the grass, pull the long reeds over us to hide again and wait. Half an hour passes. The sun is out now and I am sweating in all the wool and cotton underneath my canvas hunting jacket. I doze off. I am bored. I take my duck call out of my pocket and practice making quacking noises.

Quack Quack Quack

Craig rolls his eyes. "Stop it. You might scare them away."

I throw the call to him at the other end of the canoe. "You do it then," I say, stuffing my hands back in the deep pockets of my coat.

The next birds to come over are bluebills, and I shoot one as it is flying away over my right shoulder. The momentum of its flight carries it into the reeds behind me. Again we spend forty-five minutes looking for the bird. We don't find the bluebill either. I want to keep looking. I insist we try again. Craig says, "We'll never find it. Give it up."

The next birds to come in are wood ducks, mostly males. We shoot at them just as they have set their wings and two fall in a mess of feathers and shot, the pellets dropping like hail on the water. We paddle out to pick them up. One is breast-down in the water and when I reach down with my bare hand and pull it up by the neck, I gasp. Its breast has been shot away. I shot away its breast. The white feathers are laid wide open, dark red breast meat split open, gaping, the heart smashed, the beak smashed, the head crushed. I swallow down something nasty rising in my throat. We pick up the other wood duck and head back into the reeds. I hold the broken wood duck on my lap. What is left of its blood is soaking through my tan pants onto my long underwear. The warm heavy body lies across my knee. I am stroking this bird's elaborate, feathery purple and orange and white crest, letting tears come up to the surface and roll down my wind-chapped face.

Craig says, "Let's get the camouflage back on the boat, and then you can play."

"Play?" I ask him. At this moment I hate him fiercely. I vow that I will never hunt with him again. I wonder why I ever did. Why I married him, stayed with him. Why I hunt at all. "I'm not playing," I whisper hoarsely. Later, after we have been quiet for a time, I say to him, "Maybe you want to hunt with a man, someone who doesn't cry." He doesn't answer me.

Still later, when we are cleaning the ducks onshore and I reach my hand into the cavity of the ravaged wood duck, scraping my hand on the broken bones such that I bleed, I ask him "What would a man hunter do about this bird? Would he cry?"

Craig says, "No, he would throw it away." And there is a hardness in what he has said, so that I barely recognize his voice.

After the ducks are emptied of their hearts and livers and green, reeking, grass-filled crops, we line them up as before on the banks of the marsh and sprinkle cornmeal on them, in front of them, beside them, behind them. This time I complete the ritual with a sick resignation, as if there is nothing now that I can say or do that will make amends for this—for this hunting gone all wrong, for this hunting when the love between us has gone all wrong.

There is nothing I can do for this now, except take this wood duck home, save its skin, and give the lovely feathers to my father, who will make beautiful dry flies out of them to catch trout with in

Montana. I will salvage what breast meat I can from this wreckage and make a soup or a stew; something good to eat, something hot and rich to share with my friends, or to eat alone.

Hunting with Craig has never been like this. My heart aches and I am afraid. I hate what we have done this year. It feels like murder. In the beginning, when Craig and I were first in love, everything was different. I wonder if I will ever hunt again. I wonder if I can make sense of what has happened here. I think now that hunting for us has everything to do with love; with the way we feel about ourselves and each other. The heaviness or lightness of our hearts, our smallness or our generosity, shows in the way we hunt; in the way we treat the bluebills and mallards and teal that we shoot and eat; in the way we treat each other. I want to correct this imbalance between Craig and me and inside myself. I want to go on hunting, but not this way.

Part of what hunting meant for us, when we were together, was feasting. It wasn't the shooting that ever mattered, but what we did with this food we gathered: how we prepared the ducks to eat, how we shared them with friends, how we raised our glasses before we ate, at a long table lit by candles, covered with a lacy white cloth, and thanked the ducks for their lives. Several times a year, at Easter, at Thanksgiving and at Christmas, Craig and I prepared banquets for our friends. Nearly everything we cooked for our feasts was from our garden, or collected from the woods, or killed by us. This, I think now, was why I hunted and why I still want to. Because I want this kind of intimate relationship with the food I eat.

There were some things—flour, sugar, oranges, walnuts, chutney—that Craig and I served at our feasts that we could not

grow or collect ourselves. For these items I would shop at our local
grocery store. To get to the checkout counter in the store, I usually
walked down the meat aisle. There was hardly ever a whole animal
for sale, only parts. There were double-breasted cut-up fryers
with giblets. Three-legged fryers and the budget packs—two split
breasts with backs, two wings, two legs, two giblets, and two necks.
There were boneless, skinless thighs; packages of only drumsticks;
plastic containers of livers. There were breaded, skinless, boneless
breasts in a thin box—microwavable, 95 percent fat free, shrink-
wrapped, "all natural," and farm fresh. The meat cases were cool,
so cool I could hardly smell the meat, only a sanitary wateriness.
The smell was different from the smell of wet ducks and blood in
the bottom of our canoe. The smell was different from the smell of
the warm gut-filled cavity I reached my hand into when I cleaned
a bird. The smell was different from the smell in the kitchen
when we pulled out all the ducks' feathers, piling them up in a
soft mound on the kitchen table; different from the smell when
we dipped the birds in warm wax, wax that we then let harden and
pulled off in thick flakes along with the ducks' pinfeathers.

The birds in the store were pared down and down and down so
that what was left had no relationship to what these animals were
alive. They were birds pared down and down and down, cut and
sliced until all that was left were grotesque combinations of named
parts. It always felt obscene to me. What were these birds like
whole? It was hard, standing amid the dry coolness rising up from
the meat cases, to imagine any life; hard to construct a picture of
these birds flying, walking, making morning noise, pecking for insects in the grass, fighting over corn, laying eggs. Hard to imagine
them in any way but stacked in their airless cages.

The Russian philosopher and critic Mikhail Bakhtin tells us that the
ritual of feasting serves as a way to bridge humans' most basic fear—
fear of what Bakhtin calls "the other," fear of that which is not subject
to human control, fear of nature. In his writing about banquets and
feasting in the novels of sixteenth-century French author François
Rabelais, Bakhtin says that in the act of eating, as in the act of drinking, of making love, of giving birth, the beginning and the end of
life are linked and interwoven. In Rabelais's novels, eating celebrates
these joyful crossings or joinings, at the same time that it celebrates
the destruction of the powerful other. In feasting, the mysterious
unknown is taken into the human body; it is consumed.

One year, two weeks before Christmas, Craig and I invited twelve
of our friends to our house for a feast. We spent all day preparing
for this meal. I sliced through the dense brilliant layers of three red
cabbages and set the purple shreds to simmer in a pot with honey. I
stuffed our ducks with apples, oranges, onions, and raisins, spread
the slippery pale breasts with butter and garlic, sprinkling on
thyme and rosemary. We took handfuls of dried morel mushrooms
from a coffee can above the refrigerator, plumped them again with
white wine, sautéed them in butter.

Craig scooped out the insides of a pumpkin from the garden for
a pie. He walked to the freezer on the porch and brought back a jar
of frozen blueberries. Another pie. He took from the same freezer a
jar of cut-up frozen rhubarb. Another pie. The squash from the garden was piled in a cardboard box in the basement. I walked down
the stairs into the dark cool, collected four acorn squash, carried
them upstairs into the steamy kitchen, peeled off their tough green
and orange skins, chopped them, added butter and onions and

carrots, cooked the mixture, and pureed it for soup.

We were drinking wine and dancing as we cooked. We were full of joy. We felt generous. To feed all of these people, our friends, with food that we knew in some intimate way, food we had grown or animals we had killed ourselves, was a kind of miracle. The meal we concocted was nearly perverse in its abundance.

Appetizer: venison liver pâté and hot spiced wine.

First course: acorn squash soup sprinkled with fresh ground nutmeg.

Second course: spinach and beet green salad with chutney dressing.

Third course: barbecued venison steaks, wild rice, morel mushrooms, buttered beets, and honeyed carrots.

Fourth course: roast duck with plum gravy, new potatoes in butter and parsley sauce and sweet-and-sour red cabbage with honey, vinegar, and caraway seeds.

Dessert: rhubarb pie, blueberry pie, pumpkin pie. Ice cream.

Then brandy. Coffee. Tea. As we sat and talked, we ate tart, green and red, thinly sliced apples, slivers of pear, and cheese and grapes.

In eating these foods—these ducks that we shot out of the sky, that fell, tumbling wing overhead, with loud splashes into the cold pond beside our canoe; pumpkin pie that came from a pumpkin that grew all summer long in our backyard garden, surviving three weeks of me cutting open its stalk, scraping out squash borers with the tip of a paring knife; these mushrooms, collected over April and May in the just-leafing-out Minnesota woods full of cardinals, scarlet tanagers, bloodroot, new violets, nesting grouse, and baby rabbits; this venison, from a big-shouldered, spreading-antlered, randy buck Craig killed in November, which we tracked by following the bloody trail it left on bushes and dried grass and leaves—in eating these foods, in this passing of lives into ours, this passing of other blood and muscle into our own blood and muscle, into our own tongues and hearts; in this bridging we were taking up not only food for our bodies, but something that is wild that we wanted for ourselves. Perhaps it was our own power we were eating. Perhaps it was our own ability to grow, to shoot, to find food for ourselves, that we were eating; our ability to engage creatively with the world. We were eating what we wanted so much. We were eating life.

Audre Lorde has written about the erotic and its potential to help us redefine our relationships with ourselves, with each other, and with the world. Lorde, who died from cancer in 1992, wrote about the erotic as a way of knowing the world, as a source of power that is unlike any other source of power.

We live in a racist, patriarchal, and anti-erotic society, Lorde wrote in "Uses of the Erotic: The Erotic as Power." We live in a pornographic society that insists on the separation of so many inseparable things; that insists on ways of thinking that separate the body from the world, the body from the mind, nature from culture, men from women, black from white; a society that insists on bounded categories of difference.

But we can use erotic power to resist those splitting forces. The erotic is the sensual bridge that connects the spiritual and the political. It has to do with love. The word itself comes from the Greek word *eros*, the personification of love in all its aspects—born of chaos and personifying creative power and harmony. *Eros* is a non-rational power. *Eros* is awareness. *Eros* is not about what we do but about how acutely and fully we can feel in the doing, says Lorde. Its opposite, the pornographic, emphasizes sensation without feeling.

Pornographic relationships are those that are born not of human erotic feeling and desire, not of a love of life and a love of the body, but those relationships, those ideas, born of a fear of bodily knowledge and a desire to silence the erotic.

Everything we have ever learned in our lives tells us to suspect feeling. To doubt feeling. To doubt the power of the erotic and to confuse it, conflate it with the pornographic. But the two are at opposite ends of the world. One is about parts, not wholes. One numbs us to the irrationality, the comedy, of eating animals that are strangers to us, who come to us as perverse combinations of wings and breasts.

I understand the horror among some people I know over my shooting and eating a duck. But while I have become accustomed to hunting and eating wild duck, they are accustomed to buying and eating chicken from the store. Our actions are somehow similar yet also fundamentally different. Buying and eating a shrink-wrapped fryer feels to me like eating reduced to the necessities of time, convenience, cleanliness.

Lorde asks when we will be able, in our relationships with one another and with the world, to risk sharing the erotic's electric charge without having to look away, and without distorting the enormously powerful and creative nature of that exchange. Embracing the erotic means accepting our own mortality, our own bodiedness. Embracing the erotic means not looking away from our relationship with what we eat. And that can turn hunting into a relationship of love, at least not something brutal.

One spring I was walking around Lake of the Isles in Minneapolis with a friend. We were walking fast, dressed in sweatpants and tennis shoes. She would rather have run, but because I was recovering from knee surgery, I could only walk. We took long strides and when I stretched out my leg I could feel the scars there, the manufacturing of new tissue that gave me a strong knee.

We were talking about nothing in particular. About her job as an editor with an agricultural magazine, about running, about lifting weights, about books we had read. Suddenly I shouted, interrupting her. "Look at that."

She looked to where I was pointing and turned back to me to see what it was I was so excited about.

"Look at the ducks," I said. "All those ducks." As we came upon a gaggle of mallards, we stopped to stare. I was fascinated by the greenheads, how when they moved their heads turned violet and emerald in the light. How there was one duck there with a broken bill and a goose with only one foot. There was one female among the group of males. Two of the males were chasing her. It was mating season.

My friend and I moved on. She talked to me about her lover who teaches writing and literature at a local college. We stopped again because I'd seen a wake in the water, a silvery V streaming out behind a fast-moving muskrat. "Where?" She squinted.

"There" I said, pointing.

"What is it?"

"A muskrat," I said, watching as it moved toward a small island, its whiskered nose in the air.

I hear geese honking outside my window in the middle of the city. I used to track the garter snake in our garden from its sunny place in the bean bed to its home under the house, its entryway a piece of bent-up siding. I watch squirrels in the trash cans at the university. I pay attention to spiderwebs.

Can I call this love? Can I say that I love the swimming greenheads in Lake of the Isles, when every fall I make an adventure out
of killing them? Does killing have anything to do with love? What
kind of language allows this paradox? This tragic conflation of
violence and love is part of what I try to resist in the world, yet here
I am, in the midst of it.

How is my love for the greenheads, the swimming muskrat, the
Canada goose different from the feelings other hunters have for
the animals they kill? Can I have a relationship with these animals
alive? Or is the killing, the eating, that magical bridging, a crucial
part of my love, part of my relationship with these animals, with
the world? What does it mean, that in my body, helping to keep
me alive, to make me joyful, to share joy with people I love, is the
breast of a greenhead mallard that I shot down on a cool autumn
day and scooped from the cold water with my hand?

NATHANIEL PERRY

from
Earthly Love

Instigation in the wind,
urging winter along:
wood smoke, woodpecker, song.
One times ten is ten,

and there is one of you,
and ten things I could say.
Let's try to try it my way—
I'll tell you what is true:

movement of sun in leaves,
the breath of fall in every
thing, even things we never
notice—aftermaths, sheaves.

* * *

You are something like
a flame, something clear,
an ocean's water near
the shore, the open strike

of thunder in the air,
November stars, snow.
The smoke of days, the low
fires of night are there

inside your quiet hands.
Hold me too. I'll be quiet,
or quieter, like night
mustered at morning's command.

Traci Brimhall

Riddle at 29,000 Feet

You said marriage must sacrifice itself on the altar
of family, but this week I read about a man who

climbed back up Everest to find his missing wife.
I wash moonlight from your forehead and the Sphinx

in your chest asks again: *What comes down but never
goes up?* You never did learn how to waltz. The site

called Rainbow Valley earned its name from the bright
coats of all the climbers who never made it back

to base camp. The husband who went after his wife
is red is orange is blushing in the valley. Love is such

an unreliable savior. *What's so delicate that saying its name
breaks it?* The wife lived for two days in the cold. Saving her

was too risky, climbers said. Snow collected in her mouth.
The mountain whitened its history. She is blue is green

is singing when wind rides through her sockets. Who knows
if they had children. That's not the story. Ever, ever,

our happiness common, endurable. I ask what crazy thing
you'd do for me. Answer, the rain. Answer, silence.

CAMILLE DUNGY

Dirt

A love story

YESTERDAY, a large truck dumped seventy cubic yards of shredded cedar mulch onto our driveway. Then, because that first pile consumed more than two-thirds the driveway's available space, the truck dumped another seventy cubic yards of a compost and topsoil mixture onto the street in front of our house.

Yesterday was not a calm day. The wind has been blowing since the weekend at rates of up to forty miles an hour. The kind of wind my phone's weather app indicates with the squiggly lines I might draw under words like "very" or "so much" or "a lot." More than once, in bed the night before, I felt our house shaken by gusts. These are the kinds of winds that come to Colorado to warn us that, though we woke up on a warm day, we might go to bed blanketed in inches of snow. Yesterday was, perhaps, not the ideal day to take delivery on many hundred dollars' worth of dirt.

"Why couldn't they deliver on Friday?" my husband asked a few days ago.

"Because Wednesday is the day it is coming," I said.

Truth be told, I hadn't considered the wind when I called the landscaping supply company to arrange delivery. I'd only been focused on completing our yard project before Halloween. Now, I wanted my husband to help me make the best of a bad situation. A bad situation I might be largely responsible for creating.

As I said to our friend Tim, who happened by our house in time to watch us scramble to protect our dirt, "If this isn't a metaphor for marriage, I don't know what is."

My plan, hatched this year around Mother's Day, is to convert the lawn separating our house from our southern neighbors into a flower field that will support local pollinators. Snowy springs here often run right into the blazing heat of summer, and between a travel schedule that had me out of town nearly weekly and overseeing an interior renovation project when home, the best planting window—not to mention window of my ability to organize domestic improvement projects—slipped by.

"What are you going to do about the south lawn?" Ray wanted to know several times this summer.

"When will you get going on that flower meadow you want?" he frequently asked.

"We should get started on this project before it's too late," he warned.

I had a quiver full of excuses. It was a very hot summer. Everything was dying. I needed to do some more research on low-water, high desert plants. I wasn't in town half of June or a large chunk of August. The inside of our house was a mess. Did I want to tear up the outside of the house too? On my most exhausted days, which were many of my days, I figured it was fine if I delayed the pollinator garden project. No one uses that patch of land but for a solitary rabbit. Maybe converting the lawn to a flower field was an impractical idea.

Ray and I have been married for eleven years as of this summer. The rest of the world may experience me as the kind of person who makes decisions boldly and quickly, but for more than a decade, the reason I can do so is partly because Ray is at home patiently listening while I decide which way the wind is going to blow.

"Love is patient," a reader at our wedding reminded us.

We were married on the summer solstice, what most people think of as the longest day of the year but which some might say is the moment when the darkness starts to beat out the light. Getting married on a potently symbolic day for the planet helps us keep balance in perspective.

Ray talked to our lawn guy, a man I worried about offending with my plan to reduce the amount of lawn we'd be paying him to mow. "Andy's on board," my husband reported. "Explain what you want, and he'll come over and lend you a hand." And so, in the first part of October, Andy came with a sod cutter and cleared 280 square feet where we could amend the stripped earth until planting time comes in the spring.

The reading at our wedding declared, "Love is kind."

For about a week, I admired the weed-free stretch of hard clay, grateful to Ray for contacting Andy, and thankful to both of them for making sure my dream project was now forced under way.

My job in this project was now to call the landscaping company and arrange delivery of the elements that would help us take our next steps. This I eventually did. Without consulting the weather report, or Ray.

For several years after we moved to Colorado, my parents, who have been married fifty-five years this summer, made a habit of pointing out that when I talked about our new home, I tended to say *my* garden, *my* bedroom, *my* house. They suggested that I needed to think more carefully about how I use pronouns, as none of these spaces should be considered mine alone. This, they said, is one of the keys to sustaining a healthy and loving relationship. You need to include the other. My parents insisted that I should be thinking in terms of *our* garden, *our* bedroom, *our* home. They are correct, and I try, but too often I forget, and I slip back into thinking about what serves me alone. I was ready for the soil, and so I called for the soil, and so the soil arrived.

I found yesterday's delivery thrilling. The big truck, with its enormous, improbably shiny white compartments. The engineering feat that must have gone into figuring out how to lift that heavy bed and its otherwise secure tailgate. Each payload—but only one payload at a time—pouring into a controlled pile within feet of my front door. I loved the piles themselves, which, from out of a dust cloud, like in a magic show, emerged as mounds high and large enough to fuel a dirt-biking child's dreams. We stood by the window of my (newly renovated) home office—the driver had warned us about the dust—and I took videos and photographs while the big truck and its driver did their work.

When I showed my student Jess the video of the truck dumping an SUV-size load of soil into what appeared to be the middle of the street, she observed that—after I had finished voicing my delight, and Callie, my daughter, noted how cars were doing an admirable job of shifting course around the new road obstacle—my husband emitted what might have been the world's longest, deepest, and most exasperated sigh.

This, too, is a way of measuring love. How deep are our sighs?

How do we learn to stand by the ones who matter to us—whose interests we cannot fully fathom—even as the world dumps a pile of crap and dirt and shredded promise just outside our door?

"Can you make sure Callie gets to school on time?" Ray asked, following said sigh. "I'm going to the hardware store to buy some tarps." This was less than ninety minutes before he was expected to lecture in front of a class of a hundred students. He had papers to grade and a Keynote presentation to complete. The closest hardware store is at least thirty minutes, round trip, from our house.

Normally at that time in the morning, my husband—who, as if a male emperor penguin, often the lead parent in our home—would make sure our daughter finished her breakfast, packed her lunch, and chose socks, despite the girl's habitual aversion to wearing socks. He'd hop on his bike and trail her to the elementary school's building, then pedal off to his office. But yesterday, because his wife chose to have 140 cubic yards of dirt delivered during the windiest week we've experienced this fall, my husband had to rearrange his plans.

Let me pause here to tell you—in case you haven't gathered it already—I love this human.

"While you're at the hardware store," I hollered after my husband, "can you pick up a new spade? Or whatever you call the kind of shovel that has the pointy end."

Some people in the immediate aftermath of receiving delivery of enough landscaping material to suitably convert 280 square feet of what was formerly sod (and, let's be honest, a whole lot of dandelion, clover, crabgrass, creeping Charlie, and thistle) into an extensive native and ornamental flower garden might be hesitant to admit to their partner that they don't actually know if a shovel with a pointy end is called a spade.

Also, I understand, it is probably unreasonable that a person about to undertake such a project would have used a small, bright red, oval-ended shovel so vigorously that the shovel's head would break off in the cruel Colorado clay. Compounding these failures is the fact that only when I tried to repair the damage did I notice the words CHILDREN'S TOOLS FOR WORK AND FOR PLAY inscribed on the shovel's back end.

I realize I'm not coming off as a landscaping expert here. Sometimes, I find it hard to believe that anyone trusts me do to anything.

When we first started dating, I was in the initial stages of compiling an anthology that would come to be called *Black Nature: Four Centuries of African American Nature Poetry*. In those early days, while on a research trip to his natal city, I called Ray from Lower Manhattan. I walked on the tight, busy streets near where The Poets House used to be located. We were both living in the Bay Area at the time. Though San Francisco is a city, it's not a city like New York is a city. The densely packed buildings, bright taxis, and intimately pervasive buzz of New York made me miss the man I was beginning to love. "Where are you right now?" I asked.

He was on the fifth floor of the parking lot near our campus offices. San Francisco State University is only a few miles from the Pacific Ocean. The campus air is often heavy with salt-soaked fog.

"There's a duck on that car," said Ray.

"A duck?" I asked. Lake Merced wasn't far from campus, but I had trouble believing a duck would bother to fly all the way to the roof level of a parking garage.

"Yes. A duck. I mean, I think it's a duck." Ray stopped a bystander. "Is that a duck?"

The bird was a seagull, the bystander said. This made a lot more sense, given the proximity to the sea and the amount of trash available on campus for a seagull to scavenge.

Remember, I was in New York researching an entire book about environmentally engaged black poets. I consider myself an environmentally engaged black poet. Environmental engagement is fundamental to who I believe myself to be. And here I was, some part of me infatuated with the giant human footprint surrounding me in New York City and an even bigger part of me falling deeply in love with a New Yorker who, despite having lived in California for the better part of twenty years, still couldn't tell the difference between a seagull and a duck. He only knew it wasn't a pigeon.

Ray's bird identification skills may have been flawed, but what was more worrying to me was that, if I read the situation in one of several ways readily available, it would be possible that what I loved and how I loved them would reveal me to be an enormous, greenwashed fraud.

The duck incident, as we still call it, was a deciding factor in how my husband and I have learned to love each other. The duck incident may be one of the reasons that yesterday we had to figure out a fix for all that mulch and soil just delivered to our house in the university town in Northern Colorado where we were trying to build a more locally supportive environment, though neither of us truly knew what to do with the weather, the flora, or the unforgiving, hard, clay dirt.

I could easily have laughed at him that day on the phone call between New York and San Francisco. I mean, we both did laugh at him, and we continue to do so now. But what I mean is that I could have ridiculed him. I could have made a great deal of fun out of what he didn't know. Who confuses a duck with a seagull? They are both such recognizable birds. But I didn't ridicule him. Instead, the two of us started learning about birds together. We owned more bird identification books than baby name books by the time our daughter came into the world. We started hiking together and subscribed to the Cornell Lab of Ornithology's e-mail list. We've installed five birdfeeders in our yard already, all with different types of feed. We have an account at a store called Wild Birds Unlimited that specializes in selling seed designed specifically for the birds we find in this particular habitat. With this new plot we're converting, we plan to include a birdbath with a circulating water supply and bee and butterfly hydration stations. Thanks to the duck incident, we've become students of flying things. We've fallen more deeply in love with birds and bees and butterflies, together.

When I told my husband I didn't know the proper name for the tool I broke, he didn't laugh at me. This is part of how we say, "I love you. I love the way you help me live in the world."

When Ray and I decided to get married, he thought we should have a very small wedding. Maybe just our parents and a few of our closest friends. That wasn't what happened. By some accounts, more people were at our wedding who were friends of our parents than were personally selected friends. For this, in the end, we are grateful. One of our fondest memories was a moment during the wedding reception when the DJ invited all the married couples onto the dance floor. Then he told anyone who was married less than one day to sit down, and so, as the newlyweds, we witnessed the longevity of the relationships of the people who had come to support us.

Ray and I were married the week the state of California first issued same-sex marriage licenses, and so one of our readers and his new husband left the dance floor when the DJ said "Anyone who has been married less than five days, please take your seats." A month. Six months. A year. Two. Three. At each marker, more couples sat down. But at forty years, forty-five, even fifty-five years, couples were still smiling as they stepped in sync around the dance floor. This wedding wasn't just about us, Ray and I understood as we watched this collective motion. We'd entered a community that would help us as we worked to love each other for all our lives.

I did manage to get our kid off to school—wearing her socks even—just before Ray returned from the hardware store with two blue twenty-by-twenty-foot tarps and a shiny, new, adult-strength, pointed digging shovel. I'd heard him ask the soil delivery man what size tarps he should buy, and this is why the tarps he brought home fit our needs.

For my part, I've spent a bit of time since yesterday researching the names for different types of digging tools, forwarding the most informative article to Ray so he could share in this new set of knowledge. We're in this pursuit together, you see, learning to name the tools we need to build the kind of home we desire.

We pulled the tarps over the two piles, secured them with some broken floor tiles left over from our bathroom renovation, remaindered scraps of wood flooring, and odd pieces of lumber we found in the garage. Then, with maybe thirty minutes to spare before his class started, we got in our one car, and my husband drove us both to our jobs at the university.

Tim, the friend who stopped to see our struggles in the morning, texted both of us at three to say, "The wind has pulled your tarps back."

Ray and I both scrambled to rearrange our plans, raced home, and tried to keep the wind from claiming all our dirt and crap and mulch. We worked together—which was sweet, if a little sweaty.

The wind whipped wildly, as it often does late on fall afternoons. Drastic weather changes here can create a barometrical fuss. It's predicted that we'll get several inches of snow beginning as early as Saturday night. With that will come the snowplows, which will decimate whatever part of the topsoil pile the wind and precipitation didn't get already. Together, Ray and I shoveled into container after container some of the dirt that had stretched beyond the pile's margins and farther into the path of traffic. We kept that soil safely inside our garage until the following Saturday, when we'd hired several young men to help us move the remaining soil and mulch from the street and driveway and into the yard.

"We've passed the angle of repose," I told Ray, as the more we shoveled from the bottom of the street-side mound, the more the mound spilled back into the spots we'd just shoveled. Cars drove around us as we worked, slowing only slightly but never threatening to run us down. While Ray and I worked on saving our dirt, I kept thinking of what I'd said to our friend earlier that day, "If this isn't a metaphor for marriage, I don't know what is."

I remembered some railway ties that had been piled in the backyard. Discarded landscaping relics from the '80s. Railroad ties would do a better job securing the tarps than the leftover tiles and floorboards we'd used earlier in the day. Ray brought the heavy wood around to the front of the house in a borrowed wheelbarrow, and, together, we wrestled one by one into position.

"I don't envy you that job," said a neighbor who drove by in his green-and-white Mini Cooper. Most of the time, we can live in this world as if we are the only ones in it, but sometimes, we need to be disabused of this notion.

"The bees better never sting me again," I told Ray at some point during our windy topsoil adventure. What I meant was that the bees, to whom I am allergic, better understand that all this work we were doing was for them. Ray and I bickered about how to most efficiently get the job done, but we worked together as best we could. This wasn't about us. It was about a vision that was larger than us. How could we use less water, benefit more living beings, and build something more beautiful, more generous to our human and nonhuman neighbors, than what we'd inherited when we moved into this house? I was hoping—we were hoping—that the bees would understand the efforts we'd made to build a secure space for them, and that this recognition would be protection.

The green-and-white Mini Cooper came back as Ray and I wrangled another railroad tie onto the blue-tarped mound in the road. "Did you bring a *Cat in the Hat* cleanup machine?" I asked its driver.

"It's not much," he said, "but I looked behind my wife's she-shed and I found a few things." He offered us a couple of cinder blocks, more railroad ties, and a few heavy rocks. "Maybe these will help. Good luck!" And, rather like *The Cat in the Hat*, just as quickly as he'd come, the man was gone.

In the end, we saved nearly all the soil and mulch from the wind, and we'll lose none of it to the snowplow. Together we will make this work. Because we work well together, and because we won't be working alone. Thanks to the help of friends, family, and strangers, and with the added assistance of three borrowed wheel-barrows, a lent rake, and a variety of loaned shovels, we'll beat the snow and lay a foundation of growing material that will protect our new plot through the winter.

EVA HOOKER

Dragonfly

If shallows, if lime-rich
wetland, if muck, if bedrock
of dolomite. If she, if
underwater, if stems hold
up like tulips, all cup.
If she a circle, if
love, if he, if tail bends
like a heart, if they, if
bliss, if they fly, if wheel
about, if hooked, clear winged.
If out of harm's way, if split,
if shed, if fold their wings
above their bodies, if three
hundred eggs, if no cold
or rain, if weave, dodge,
hover, if eat, if soft
mosquito, if sun—

then bog dancer, amber
wing, blue pirate, raggedy
skimmer, spinylegged clubtail,
green darner—

if sun

D U Y D O A N

Lake Hoàn Kiếm

The wind plays with the moon; the moon with the wind.
The moon sets. Who can the wind play with?
            —Vietnamese folk song, translation by John Balaban

Meet me on the unlit stretch of lake least fooled
by autumn. Under the youngest willow.

Its thin branches hang over me, its leaves
veil my face from the milk flower playing
matchmaker.

You say you love her sweet scent.
Even the plum blossom isn't so lavish.

One day I will take a wife myself.
If I reach forward, I can touch the water
past the edge of the moon.

I wait for you beyond the temple lights
at the center of the lake, my ankles deep
in a pillar of moon on the water.

Come whisper our secrets to the lake,
make it shiver in unison with the willow.
Shall we become now
worthy of the Lạc-Hồng race?

SCOTT RUSSELL SANDERS

Beauty

IN MEMORY, I wait beside Eva in the vestibule of the church to play my bit part as father of the bride. She hooks a hand on my elbow while three bridesmaids fuss over her, fixing the gauzy veil, spreading the long ivory train of her gown, tucking into her bun a loose strand of hair, which glows the color of honey filled with sunlight. Clumsy in my rented patent leather shoes and stiff black tuxedo, I stand among these gorgeous women like a crow among doves. I realize they're gorgeous not because they carry bouquets or wear silk dresses, but because the festival of marriage has slowed time down until any fool can see their glory.

Concerned that we might walk too fast, as we did in rehearsal, Eva tries in vain to teach me a gliding ballet step to use as we process down the aisle.

"It's really simple, Daddy," she says, as I botch it over and over.

I fear that I will stagger along beside my elegant daughter like a veteran wounded in foreign wars.

Eva, meanwhile, seems blissfully confident, not only of being able to walk gracefully, as she could do in her sleep, but of standing before this congregation and solemnly promising to share her life with Matthew Allen, the man who waits in thinly disguised turmoil at the far end of the aisle. Poised on the dais, wearing a black

ministerial robe and a white stole, is the good friend whom Eva
and I know best as our guide on canoe trips through the Boundary
Waters. He grins so broadly that his full cheeks push up against the
round rims of his spectacles.

"There's one happy preacher," Eva says.

"He believes in marriage," I reply.

"So do I. Remember, Matt and I figured that between you and
Mom and his folks, our parents have been married fifty-eight years."

Eva lets go of my arm to lift a hand to her throat, touching the
string of pearls she has borrowed from my own bride, Ruth, to
whom I've been married thirty years.

Love may last, I want to say, but don't, feeling unsure of my
voice. Eva returns her free hand to my arm and tightens her grip.
The arm she holds is my left one, close against my racing heart. In
her own left arm she balances a great sheaf of flowers—daisies and
lilies, marigolds, snapdragons, bee balm, feverfew—and in her left
hand she holds a Belgian lace handkerchief, also borrowed from
Ruth, in case she cries.

The organ strikes up Bach's "Jesu, Joy of Man's Desiring" for
the bridesmaids' entrance, and down the aisle they skim, those gorgeous women in midnight blue. Overawed by the crowd, the flower
girls hang back until their mother nudges them along, and then
they dash and skip, carrying their fronds of flowers like spears.

Finally, only the bride and the father of the bride remain in the
vestibule. Eva whispers, "Remember, now, don't walk too fast."
But how can I walk slowly while my heart races? I've forgotten the
ballet step she tried to show me. I want events to pause so I can
practice the step, so we can go canoeing once more in the wilderness, so we can sit on a boulder by the sea and talk over life's

mysteries, so I can make up to my darling for anything she may
have lacked in her girlhood. But events do not pause. The organ
sounds the first few bars of Purcell's "Trumpet Voluntary," our
cue to show ourselves. We move into the open doorway, and two
hundred faces turn their lit eyes on us. Eva tilts her face up at me,
quirks the corners of her lips into a tight smile, and says, "Here we
go, Daddy." And so, lifting our feet in unison, we go.

The wedding took place in Bloomington, Indiana, hometown for
Matthew as well as Eva, on a sizzling Saturday in July. Now in
early September, I can summon up hundreds of details from that
radiant day, but on the day itself I was aware only of a surpassing
joy. The glow of happiness had to cool before it would crystallize
into memory.

Pardon my cosmic metaphor, but I can't help thinking of the
physicists' claim that, if we trace the universe back to its origins
in the Big Bang, we find the multiplicity of things fusing into
greater and greater simplicity, until at the moment of creation itself there is only pure undifferentiated energy. Without being able
to check their equations, I think the physicists are right. I believe
the energy they speak of is holy, by which I mean it is the closest
we can come with our instruments to measuring the strength
of God. I also believe this primal energy continues to feed us,
directly through the goods of creation, and indirectly through the
experience of beauty. The thrill of beauty is what entranced me
as I stood with Eva's hand hooked over my arm while the Wedding March played, as it entrances me on these September nights
when I walk over dewy grass among the songs of crickets and
stare at the Milky Way.

We're seeing the Milky Way, and every other denizen of the sky, far more clearly these days thanks to the sharp eyes of the Hubble Space Telescope, as it orbits out beyond the blur of Earth's atmosphere. From data beamed down by the telescope, for example, I summon onto my computer screen an image of Jupiter wrapped in its bands of cloud like a ball of heathery yarn. Then I call up the Cat's Eye Nebula, incandescent swirls of red looped around the gleam of a helium star, for all the world like the burning iris of a tiger. This fierce glare began its journey toward Earth 3,000 years ago, about the time my Assyrian ancestors were in their prime. Bushing back deeper in time, I summon onto my screen the Eagle Nebula, 7,000 light-years away, a trio of dust clouds like rearing horses, their dark bodies scintillating with the sparks of newborn stars. I study images of quasars giving birth to galaxies, galaxies whirling in the shapes of pinwheels, supernovas ringed by strands of luminous debris, and all the while I'm delving back toward that utter beginning when you and I and my daughter and her new husband and the bright heavenly host were joined in the original burst of light.

On these cool September mornings, I've been poring over two sets of photographs, those from deep space and those from Eva's wedding, trying to figure out why such different images—of supernova and shining daughter, of spinning galaxies and trembling bouquets—set up in me the same hum of delight. The feeling is unusually intense for me just now, so soon after the nuptials, but it has never been rare. As far back as I can remember, things seen or heard or smelled, things tasted or touched, have provoked in me an answering vibration. The stimulus might be the sheen of

moonlight on the needles of a white pine, or the iridescent glimmer on a dragonfly's tail, or the lean silhouette of a ladder-back
chair, or the glaze on a hand-thrown pot. It might be birdsong or a
Bach sonata or the purl of water over stone. It might be a line of poetry, the outline of a cheek, the savor of bread, the sway of a bough
or a bow. The provocation might be as grand as a mountain sunrise
or as humble an icicle's jeweled tip, yet in each case a familiar
surge of gratitude and wonder wells up in me.

Now and again some voice raised on the stairs leading to my
study, some passage of music, some noise from the street, will stir
a sympathetic thrum from the strings of the guitar that tilts against
the wall behind my door. Just so, over and over again, impulses from
the world stir a responsive chord in me — not just any chord, but a
particular one, combining notes of elegance, exhilaration, simplicity,
and awe. The feeling is as recognizable to me, as unmistakable, as
the sound of Ruth's voice or the beating of my own heart. A screech
owl calls, a comet streaks the night sky, a story moves unerringly to a
close, a child lays an arrowhead in the palm of my hand, my daughter smiles at me through her bridal veil, and I feel for a moment at
peace, in place, content. I sense in those momentary encounters
a harmony between myself and whatever I behold. The word that
seems to fit most exactly this feeling of resonance, this sympathetic
vibration between inside and outside, is *beauty*.

What am I to make of this resonant feeling? Do my sensory
thrills tell me anything about the world? Does beauty reveal a
kinship between my small self and the great cosmos, or does my
desire for meaning only fool me into thinking so? Perhaps, as biologists maintain, in my response to patterns I'm merely obeying
the old habits of evolution. Perhaps, like my guitar, I'm only

a sounding box played on by random forces.

I must admit that two cautionary sayings keep echoing in my head. Beauty is only skin-deep, I've heard repeatedly, and beauty is in the eye of the beholder. Appealing surfaces may hide ugliness, true enough, as many a handsome villain or femme fatale should remind us. The prettiest of butterflies and mushrooms and frogs include some of the most poisonous ones. It's equally true that our taste may be influenced by our upbringing, by training, by cultural fashion. One of my neighbors plants in his yard a pink flamingo made of translucent plastic and a concrete goose dressed in overalls, while I plant in my yard oxeye daisies and jack-in-the-pulpits and maidenhair ferns, and both of us, by our own lights, are chasing beauty.

Mustn't beauty be shallow if it can be painted on? Mustn't beauty be a delusion if it can blink off and on like a flickering bulb? A wedding gown will eventually grow musty in a mothproof box. Flowers will fade, and the glow will seep out of the brightest day. I'll grant that we may be fooled by facades, may be led astray by our fickle eyes. But I've been married to Ruth for thirty years, remember. I've watched my daughter grow for twenty-four years, my son for twenty, and these loved ones have taught me a more hopeful possibility. Season after season I've knelt over fiddleheads breaking ground, studied the wings of swallowtails nectaring on blooms, spied skeins of geese high in the sky. There are books I've read, pieces of music I've listened to, ideas I've revisited time and again with fresh delight. Having lived among people and places and works of imagination whose beauty runs all the way through, I feel certain that genuine beauty is more than skin deep, that real beauty dwells not in my own eye alone but out in the world.

While I can speak with confidence of what I feel in the presence of beauty, I must go out on a speculative limb if I'm to speak about the qualities in the world that call it forth. Far out on that limb, therefore, let me suggest that a creature, an action, a landscape, a line of poetry or music, a scientific formula, or anything else that might seem beautiful, seems so because it gives us a glimpse of the underlying order of things. The swirl of a galaxy and the swirl of a gown resemble one another not merely by accident, but because they follow the grain of the universe. That grain runs through our own depths. What we find beautiful accords with our most profound sense of how things *ought* to be. Ordinarily, we live in a tension between our perceptions and our desires. When we encounter beauty, that tension vanishes, and outward and inward images agree.

Before I climb out any farther onto this limb, let me give biology its due. It may be that in pursuing beauty we're merely obeying our genes. It may be that the features we find beautiful in men or women, in art or landscape or weather, are ones that improved the chances of survival for our ancestors. Put the other way around, it's entirely plausible that the early humans who did *not* tingle at the sight of a deer, the smell of a thunderstorm, the sound of running water, or the stroke of a hand on a shapely haunch, all died out, carrying with them their oblivious genes.

Who can doubt that biology, along with culture, plays a crucial role in tuning our senses? The gravity that draws a man and woman together, leading each to find the other ravishing, carries with it a long history of sexual selection, one informed by a shrewd calculation of fertility and strength. I remember how astonished I

was to realize, one rainy spring day in seventh grade, that the girl
sitting in the desk beside me was suddenly, enormously *interesting*.
My attention was riveted on Mary Kay's long blonde hair, which
fell in luxuriant waves over the back of her chair, until it brushed
against a rump that swelled, in a way I had never noticed before,
her green plaid skirt. As a twelve-year-old, I would not have called
Mary Kay beautiful, although I realize now that is what she was.
And I would have balked at the suggestion that my caveman ancestors had any say in my dawning desire, although now I can hear
their voices grunting. Go for the lush hair, the swelling rump.

If we take a ride through the suburbs and study the rolling acres
of lawn dotted with clumps of trees and occasional ponds, what do we
see but a faithful simulation of the African savanna where humans
first lived? Where zoning laws permit, the expanse of green will often
be decorated by grazing animals, docile and fat, future suppers on
the hoof. The same combination of watering holes, sheltering trees,
and grassland shows up in paintings and parks the world over, from
New Delhi to New York. It is as though we shape our surroundings to
match an image, coiled in our DNA, of the bountiful land.

Perhaps in every case, as in our infatuation with lover or landscape, a sense of biological fitness infuses the resonant, eager,
uplifting response to the world that I am calling beauty. Yet I persist
in believing there is more to this tingle than an evolutionary reflex.
Otherwise, how could a man who is programmed to lust after every
nubile female nonetheless be steadily attracted, year after year, to
the same woman? Why would I plant my yard with flowers that I
cannot eat?

As far back as we can trace our ancestors, we find evidence
of a passion for design—decorations on pots, beads on clothes,

pigments on the ceilings of caves. Bone flutes have been found at human sites dating back more than thirty thousand years. So we answer the breathing of the land with our own measured breath; we answer the beauty we find with the beauty we make. Our ears may be finely tuned for detecting the movements of predators or prey, but that does not explain why we should be so moved by listening to Gregorian chants or Delta blues. Our eyes may be those of a slightly reformed ape, trained for noticing whatever will keep skin and bones intact, but that scarcely explains why we should be so enthralled by the lines of a Shaker chair or a Dürer engraving, or by photographs of Jupiter.

As it happens, Jupiter is the brightest light in the sky on these September evenings, blazing in the southeast at dusk. Such a light must have dazzled our ancestors long before telescopes began to reveal the planet's husk of clouds or its halo of moons. We know that night-watchers in many cultures kept track of the heavenly dance because the records of their observations have come down to us. Did they watch so faithfully because they believed the stars and planets controlled their fate, or because they were mesmerized by the majesty of the night? I can't speak for them. But when I look at Jupiter, with naked eye or binoculars, or in the magnified images broadcast down from the Hubble Telescope, I am not looking for a clue to the morning's weather or to the mood of a deity, any more than I am studying the future of my genes when I gaze at my daughter. I am looking for the sheer bliss of looking.

In a wedding scene that has cooled into memory from the red glow of happiness, I keep glancing at Eva's face as we process down the aisle, trying to match my gawky stride to her graceful one. The light on her skin shimmers through the veil. A ripple of voices follows us toward the altar, like the sound of waves breaking on cobbles. The walk seems to go on forever, but it also seems to be over far too soon. Ready or not, we take our place at center stage, with the bridesmaids in midnight blue to our left, Matthew and his grooms-men in black to our right. My heart thrashes like a bird in a sack.

The minister, our canoeing guide, gives us both a steadying glance. Then he lifts his voice to inquire of the hushed congrega-tion, "Who blesses this marriage?"

I swallow to make sure my own voice is still there, and say loudly, "The families give their blessing."

I step back, lift Eva's hand from my arm and place it on Mat-thew's, a gesture that seemed small in rehearsal yesterday but that seems huge today. Then my bit part is over. I leave the stage, care-fully stepping around the long train of Eva's dress, and go to my seat beside Ruth, who dabs a handkerchief to her eyes. I grasp her free hand so deft and familiar. Just one month shy of thirty years after my own wedding, I want to marry her all over again. Despite my heart's mad thrashing, I haven't felt like crying until this mo-ment, as I sit here beside my own bride, while Eva recites her vows with a sob in her throat. When I hear that sob, tears rise in me, but joy rises more swiftly.

Judging from the scientists I know, including Eva and Ruth, and those whom I've read about, you can't pursue the laws of nature very long without bumping into beauty. "I don't know if it's the same beauty you see in the sunset," a friend tells me, "but it *feels* the same." This friend is a physicist, who has spent a long career deciphering what must be happening in the interior of the stars.

He recalls for me his thrill on grasping for the first time Dirac's equations describing quantum mechanics, or those of Einstein describing relativity. "They're so beautiful," he says, "you can see immediately they have to be true. Or at least on the way toward truth." I ask him what makes a theory beautiful, and he replies, "Simplicity, symmetry, elegance, and power."

Why nature should conform to theories we find beautiful is far from obvious. The most incomprehensible thing about the universe, as Einstein said, is that it's comprehensible. How unlikely, that a short-lived biped on a two-bit planet should be able to gauge the speed of light, lay bare the structure of an atom, or calculate the gravitational tug of a black hole. We're a long way from understanding everything, but we do understand a great deal about how nature behaves. Generation after generation, we puzzle out formulas, test them, and find, to an astonishing degree, that nature agrees. An architect draws designs on flimsy paper, and her buildings stand up through earthquakes. We launch a satellite into orbit and use it to bounce messages from continent to continent. The machine on which I write these words embodies hundreds of insights into the workings of the material world, insights that are confirmed by every burst of letters on the screen, and I stare at that screen through lenses that obey the laws of optics first worked out in detail by Isaac Newton.

By discerning patterns in the universe, Newton believed, he was tracing the hand of God. Scientists in our day have largely abandoned the notion of a Creator as an unnecessary hypothesis, or at least an untestable one. While they share Newton's faith that the universe is ruled everywhere by a coherent set of rules, they cannot say, as scientists, how these particular rules came to govern things.

You can do science without believing in a divine Legislator, but not without believing in laws.

I spent my teenage years scrambling up the mountain of mathematics. Midway up the slope, however, I staggered to a halt, gasping in the rarefied air, well before I reached the heights where the equations of Einstein and Dirac would have made sense. Nowadays I add, subtract, multiply, and do long division when no calculator is handy, and I can do algebra and geometry and even trigonometry in a pinch, but that is about all that I've kept from the language of numbers. Still, I remember glimpsing patterns in mathematics that seemed as bold and beautiful as a skyful of stars.

I'm never more aware of the limitations of language than when I try to describe beauty. Language can create its own loveliness, of course, but it cannot deliver to us the radiance we apprehend in the world, any more than a photograph can capture the stunning swiftness of a hawk or the withering power of a supernova. Eva's wedding album holds only a faint glimmer of the wedding itself. All that pictures or words can do is gesture beyond themselves toward the fleeting glory that stirs our hearts. So I keep gesturing.

"All nature is meant to make us think of paradise," Thomas Merton observed. Because the Creation puts on a nonstop show, beauty is free and inexhaustible, but we need training in order to perceive more than the most obvious kinds. Even fifteen billion years or so after the Big Bang, echoes of that event still linger in the form of background radiation, only a few degrees above absolute zero. Just so, I believe, the experience of beauty is an echo of the order and power that permeate the universe. To measure background radiation, we need subtle instruments; to measure beauty, we need alert intelligence and our five keen senses.

Anyone with eyes can take delight in a face or a flower. You need training, however, to perceive the beauty in mathematics or physics or chess, in the architecture of a tree, the design of a bird's wing, or the shiver of breath through a flute. For most of human history, the training has come from elders who taught the young how to pay attention. By paying attention, we learn to savor all sorts of patterns, from quantum mechanics to patchwork quilts.

This predilection brings with it a clear evolutionary advantage, for the ability to recognize patterns helped our ancestors to select mates, find food, avoid predators. But the same advantage would apply to all species, and yet we alone compose symphonies and crossword puzzles, carve stone into statues, map time and space. Have we merely carried our animal need for shrewd perceptions to an absurd extreme? Or have we stumbled onto a deep congruence between the structure of our minds and the structure of the universe?

I am persuaded the latter is true. I am convinced there's more to beauty than biology, more than cultural convention. It flows around and through us in such abundance, and in such myriad forms, as to exceed by a wide margin any mere evolutionary need. Which is not to say that beauty has nothing to do with survival: I think it has everything to do with survival. Beauty feeds us from the same source that created us. It reminds us of the shaping power that reaches through the flower stem and through our own hands. It restores our faith in the generosity of nature. By giving us a taste of the kinship between our own small minds and the great Mind of the Cosmos, beauty reassures us that we are exactly and wonderfully made for life on this glorious planet, in this magnificent universe. I find in that affinity a profound source of meaning and hope. A universe so prodigal of beauty may actually need us to notice and respond, may need our sharp eyes and brimming hearts and teeming minds, in order to close the circuit of Creation.

KATHLEEN DEAN MOORE

Shy Affectionate SF

MY HUSBAND is a self-described "hard" scientist. He studies chemicals in the brain—how desire actually works in the cells. He listens to me talk about what it means to love a place, but says I can't just assume that people care about places. He says I need data.

"I'm a philosopher," I tell him. "Philosophers don't do data."

But the fact is, I have been conducting a study of sorts. For several months I have been reading the love ads in the local Saturday paper. The secret, coded yearnings, the SWFs and DMs all ISO, in search of, something—this interested me. I never had the occasion or even the temptation to phone the Lonesome Horseman or send a photo to Teddy Bear or tell Endangered Species that I'm a rarity myself, but I was curious. Love ads are a data bank of human nature far more revealing than the Human Genome Project: fifty people every week explaining who they are and what they are looking for, in twenty-five words or less.

I kept a count of the love ads in the *Corvallis Gazette-Times*, tallying up what people were searching for. The typical SF, a LARGE & BEAUTIFUL momma, thirty-one, who is shy and honest, likes the outdoors, movies, and walking on the beach, in that order. The typical SM is a VERY FIT MALE, who is also very sensitive. He likes the outdoors, romance, and tattoos, again, in that order. In all, fully two-thirds of the SFs and SMs put the outdoors first on their lists.

After the outdoors, the runner-up was watching movies. Beaches and camping tied for third place. Walks and hikes came in fourth. Then came dancing and dinner, followed by romance. (Notice how long it has taken to get to romance—sixth on the list.) After romance, there was a three-way tie among cuddling, fishing, and country-western music, although none of the people who liked to cuddle also liked to fish, and there was one vote each for mountains, darkness, blues, Harleys, hand-holding, friendship, and vampires. My research found no significant difference between men and women, except that three women liked sports, which are evidently of no interest whatsoever to the men. So there it is. People like the outdoors best of all, they say, better even than sex.

My husband received these data with astonishment and chagrin. "Kathy, this is bad science." I know that, but that doesn't mean it isn't important. I don't claim that everybody loves the outdoors; I just want to point out that many people do, and that love for place and love for people are mixed together in beautiful and mysterious ways. It's significant that, more often than not, when people envision their unlived lives, imagine starting over and doing it right this time, the outdoors is the setting for their dreams. Big-Hearted Bob and Chantilly Lace walking hand in hand at the edge of the sea: the raised pulse, the rhythmic waves, the salty, exultant wind.

In 1984 Harvard entomologist E. O. Wilson advanced the biophilia hypothesis, arguing that humans have an innate attraction to living things. I like this hypothesis. It offers hope: if human beings naturally love the living things on this planet, then maybe we can find a way to act lovingly toward them.

That is why I was happy to present my husband with evidence consistent with Wilson's hypothesis, and to suggest one more thing. Read the love ads closely: "ISO LTR." In search of a long-term relationship. The people who place ads in my hometown newspaper aren't just advertising for partners. What they seek is lasting relationship—with people and the planet—and what they cherish is a caring connection with a person and a place. We are creatures who are born to love. It's more than biophilia that drives us. It's philophilia—the love of love itself.

DEBORAH DENICOLA

This Morning from the Porch

Unbearable brilliance. Each leaf surrendering
to the late ceremony of sun.
The neighbor's tomato plants have fallen
through the slats in the white fence
and in the breeze, there's no denying autumn.
I keep my windows open despite the chill.

This afternoon I read how Blake thought man was bound
to the worm since God created Adam from clay and earth.
His painting shows Elohim's hands on Adam's head,
both their expressions, contorted and tormented.

From across the street tonight a child hollers twenty times
Nobody likes me, Nobody likes me—All day I have not spoken;
so I call from my window *I do, I do!* Though I'm not sure
which child it is that cried or for how long I could abide him.

I think of Blake's dark red colour print, the huge serpent
wound around Adam's legs. Creation then, is spirit
trapped in form, the first stage of the fall.

When the lousy movie on TV ends with a brutal death,
I stand by the window weeping into the cicadas.
Something palpable rises and multiplies in the darkness.

My love does not mean less because there is no lover.
It might mean more in the forgiveness of its losses.
Free-floating between breaths, it deepens down to the worm.
I remember Adam's dark red fruit and the struggle up from mud.

I cry for summer's end and for the child no one likes.
For humankind and the green world's serpents.
I am crying because I cannot bear imagining more love.

TEDDY MACKER

The Kingdom of God

A meditation

IN A FAMILIAR MUDRA, a downstretched right hand, the Buddha touches the earth. What is the meaning of this gesture?

Another day alive. Down at the field, in the afternoon's whitest heat, my friend snaps open a cucumber. "It's like drinking a glass of water," he says.

Robert Louis Stevenson is walking down a street in Pitlochry when he sees a man kicking a dog. He grabs the man by the arm, yanks him away. "What're you doing?" the man sputters. "That's my dog!" "That's not your dog," Stevenson replies. "That's God's dog."

There are, some scientists say, five thousand different types of fireflies.

You can see my baby's heartbeat in the soft spot of her skull.

America has more shopping malls, says the bumper sticker, than high schools.

Every eleven years another billion people.

The Buddha was born under a tree, attained enlightenment under a tree, and died under a tree. *Shakyamuni* translates to "Sage of the Oak Tree People." When Jesus was approaching Jericho, crowds gathered at the road, but Zacchaeus, short, could not see Him. So Zacchaeus climbed a sycamore. "Zacchaeus," Christ said, looking up into the branches, "I would like to stay at your house."

It is another day and the suffering of this world continues. A mother pig shitting in the chute. A woman dodging stones.

In the last two hundred years the United States has lost 50 percent of its wetlands, 90 percent of its old-growth forests in the Northwest, and 99 percent of its tallgrass prairies. Martin Rees, England's Astronomer Royal and professor at Cambridge, gives mankind fifty-fifty odds of making it to 2100. This world, says an old Sanskrit poet, was made long ago by good men with big hearts; some sustained it while others subdued it and gave it away as if it were straw.

The other night, through the closed door, I heard my wife singing "The Rose" to hush our baby. At first I was tickled by her wobbly voice and the maudlin quality of the scene—but, listening more, I soon found myself totally undefended. Who was this woman in the bathroom? Who was she?

May my conscience hurt me into grace.

May the bees of attention fill the clear comb of the present.

May my knees know wood.

In Russia, a friend tells me, there are young girls who carve turnips into small coffins to bury flies. Hearing this calls to mind other great Artists of Life: Henry David Thoreau scenting his handkerchief with an apple spray, the bride stepping through the jungle at night wearing an anklet of fireflies, Ryokan drinking sake with the farmers till all their eyebrows turn white with snow; calls to mind the pen and paper along the sill of the outhouse, the portrait of the wife painted on the inside of the medieval shield, and the woman who woke me from a nap so many years ago, a nap on a summer day, fanning my sleeping face with the front of her dress.

If I were to quit worrying about what others thought of me, friends and family in particular, how much more time would I have in my day to do a reverence, do right by this world? "What is clarity of mind?" a monk asks a master. "If two thousand people call to you," he replies, "and you don't look back."

In the alms of this moment, the mother stillness of the barn.

In the alms of this moment, the humble scornless million hands of water.

The moon has not yet risen, the bed is warm with my wife. No obstacles in my heart, everything a frail-boned kindness.

In the alms of this moment, the whirling quiet of a resting thigh.

In the alms of this moment, the exactful mystery of a baby's pink curling toes.

With my little knowledge, I have known, a handful of times, the greater knowledge. Once it happened standing shin deep in the Big Sur River, cobbles clattering at my feet.

In the alms of this moment, red hairline deltas on a woman's closed eyes.

Live close to the bone, suggests Thoreau. Live a single-gourd life, says the Chinese poet. A trunk and two handbags, offers D. H. Lawrence, are more than enough. And Jesus? Don't even bring along your stave. Buddha? Buddha scavenged rags from the graves of executed convicts.

In the alms of this moment, the lilac underside of a trout.

It is Lu Yu who perhaps moves me the most, the spirit attuned to the local pleasure, the little here, the life undistracted, the wonder. In my favorite poem of his he tells us his garden might be small but still it has yellow and purple plums . . . "What it all is," another poet once wrote, "I know not, but with gratitude the tears fall."

In a familiar mudra, a downstretched right hand, the Buddha touches the earth. What could be the meaning of this gesture? Later he will exhort followers to cease travel during the rainy season to avoid stepping on worms.

The train passes and I notice my wife's little hoop earring on the windowsill.

Crippled with joy, I see my daughter's gummy smile.

Once I stood shin deep in the Big Sur River, cobbles clattering at my feet.

TOM CRAWFORD

Prayer

I'm cutting my swallows from black silk,
China's best, Father, so that when flying
they meet with the least amount of resistance
and thank you again for the abundance
of insects over the green rice fields
this evening, the water bumpy with frog eyes
reflecting a pink west flowing sky

Now I'm sewing into the material
my red heart because the dead, lately,
have been a little noisy in my sleep
and about this prayer. Father,
I don't want any confusion —

I'm mud deep here
in love and would like to stay on
a while longer at least until I get the sun right,
its light over the rim of this bowl
we all eat from, and to watching,
while I'm at it, the little spot fires

appearing over the back of my hands —
my age, a quiet invitation
to bird watching
where light around the grey heron,
alone in the water,
dies down, in time, to black,
and what the imagination can rescue.

David James Duncan

Assailed

Improvisations in the key of cosmology

for Annie Dillard, in avid correspondence
with whom these improvs were conceived

Journal Entry

The countless things that fit in our minds and imaginations do
so because they are abstract. Abstraction, in this sense, is highly
useful: it is what makes memories and knowledge portable; art,
science, and stories possible; and music, images, and experiences
had or heard by a "you" capable of moving through time and space
into a "me."

The danger of abstraction is that the matter and life-forms that
surround and sustain us are not abstract. Our actions unleash
forces latent in abstract concepts upon the realm of matter and
living forms. These concepts, if insufficiently faithful to life, cause
harm. This is why we need cosmologies. Cosmology is creation and
abstraction engaged in imaginative negotiation; it is mind, matter,
and spirit at play.

When the cosmos speaks to us, it does not use words. We are
all involved, daily, in translating creation's nonverbal messages

into abstract thought and language. To live in harmony with other life-forms and one another, our translations must be accurate. If, for instance, we flout the cosmologists known as meteorologists and wear shorts and a T-shirt at ten below, we freeze; if we defy the cosmologists known as soil scientists and irrigate with alkaline water, our gardens wither; if we flout the cosmologists who study pollutants and power cities with coal-fired electricity, we fill the air, clouds, rain, soil, rivers, foods with a host of evils, and thousands unnecessarily suffer and die.

A cosmological story, though built of abstract language, must accurately translate the living here and now. Stories too literally rooted in tradition lose this accuracy. In Leviticus 14, Moses urges the rabbis of his day to end outbreaks of epidemic disease by catching two birds, killing one of them, and washing the infected person's house with both the living bird's body and the dead bird's blood. To worship such a scripture by literalizing it dishonors scripture's life-giving intent, dooms the diseased, and needlessly kills birds.

Moses was a living man, not a walking, talking compendium of archaic dos and don'ts. His cosmology was an ongoing series of creative responses to ever-changing circumstance. And for all his wisdom, Moses had a famously short fuse. When I picture him learning that human industry is pushing five or six Hiroshima bombs' worth of heat into the atmosphere every second, or that we've lost huge portions of the polar caps that give us viable seasons and the oceans' life-giving gyres, turning the seven seas into equivalents of the North Pacific's nearly currentless and lifeless "blob," or that, if unchecked, our industry will set off planet-warming chain reactions that make Earth uninhabitable to every life-form named in Genesis including Moses's people, it's hard to imagine that old defender of the holy wouldn't summit Capitol Hill and issue a freshly graven list of *thou shalt nots* that would leave coal plants, tar sands, fracking, and internal combustion to be dealt with as the abominations they have become.

A living cosmology inhales what's life-engendering and exhales what's lethal; it cross-pollinates or migrates when needed, morphs, reasons, and intuits as needed; imagines and responds as needed. The best cosmological speculation, it therefore seems to me, unfolds in a manner more like an improvised raga or jazz tune than the classical recital of a long-existing composition. A jazz pianist or Indian sitarist can, on any given occasion, pull trained instincts from their fingers and mercurial structures from their mind, interact with keyboard or fret board, and extemporaneously produce music utterly unique to time and place. Shouldn't the possessor of a viable cosmology be able to do the same?

I live in the extreme upper Columbia River drainage, in the Bitterroot Mountains' rain shadow, in a cottonwood and willow creek bottom between five-thousand- to six-thousand-foot elevation ridges. We call the year 2002 and the season "spring." Can I extemporaneously pull trained instincts from my fingers and structures from my mind and heart and improvise a series of cosmological riffs based on what is materially and spiritually perceptible here and now, moving through time and space with me, true to what I see, hear, feel, dream, and intuit this day?

Assignment: sit down and find out.

Improvisation #1: Stars, Cells, Snow
It is March in Montana and the door between Winter and Spring is

swinging violently. For days, a sometimes gentle, sometimes brutal southwesterly wind has been breaking over the Bitterroot Mountains, bringing walls of cloud so vast and near black they look world ending. Each dark wall dumps a load of snow. An impossibly blue sky then breaks out. The snow grows blinding, melts, birds burst into arias, summer feels just round the corner. Then—tied to the balm like an anti-proverbial March lion to its lamb—the next cloud wall appears, seeming to hurtle the world back an entire season.

Studying this weather as I drive home after taking my daughters to school, I go to my desk to work, and see that after a winter of literary labors it looks as if the same wild March weather has been blasting through my study. Setting work aside, I fetch a dust cloth and large cardboard box and set out to restore order. An hour into this operation I start to recycle two old magazines—a *Time*, a *National Geographic*—but first open the *Time* to save a grouse-feather bookmark. The page the feather marked stops me in my tracks.

It's a Hubble Space Telescope photo of clouds in the Orion Nebula. They're fifteen hundred light-years (that's 10,000,000,000,000,000,000 miles) from Montana and me. They're made not of ice crystals, like the clouds outside, but of superheated hydrogen that lights them from within. In color they range from orange to gold to rosewood brown, pierced here and there by tiny flares of blazing pink. In form they're flagrantly phallic, and remind me of stalagmites, velvet moose antlers, coral formations, basalt stacks on the lower Columbia River and, begging our pardon, one of the exceedingly odd parts of Everyman. In size, however, the Orion clouds annihilate all earthly analogy: they are *6 trillion miles long.*

There are projections coming off them. Shaped like animal ears, bean sprouts, the antennae of slugs, some of them artfully tipped by the striking pink flares, the protuberances are tiny compared to the masses out of which they protrude. Yet even the smallest, the Hubble astronomers tell us, are as wide as our entire solar system, and even the smallest contain something astounding: *stars*.

Those piercingly pink flares? They're fetal stars, caught by the Hubble camera in the very process of being born. What's more, the astronomers tell us, our sun, solar system, Earth, its hydrogen, oxygen, water, and life-forms, you and I included, are all the offspring of these same kind of clouds. For the first time in my life it hits me: the sun, Earth, and I are siblings. Despite our obvious endless differences, we're each the progeny of just such stupendous clouds. As I sit by my Montana window, I'm seated in the light of an Ancient Brother, on the lap of an Ancient Sister, looking, as if in a family album, at a photo of our 6-trillion-mile-long heavenly Father/Mothers. This gives me a feeling so paradoxical it makes me dizzy. I am so tiny and short-lived compared to the Orion parent-clouds I can find no words appropriate to my insignificance. Yet I share a progenitive shape with them; I have conceived offspring as have they, and my offspring shine like stars to me.

An uncanny fact from a book I've been reading, Sara Maitland's *A Joyful Theology*: the number of cells in the human body is close to the same as the number of stars in the Milky Way. Is this meaningless coincidence or a purposeful symmetry devised by our Creator? I have no idea. I only know that some facts make me happy, and that a flurry of such facts have been set awhirl.

Fact: the spring day has darkened and snow is swirling and falling again.

Fact: a contradictorily bright feeling is swirling through me.

Facts: I am sitting amid mountains, pondering a celestial cloud whose "snow" is stars and a terrestrial cloud whose "stars" are snow; my children and I each have a Milky Way's worth of cells burning in our bodies; and our galaxy has a human being's worth of star-cells shining within its vast gyre.

Improvisation #2: True Wilderness

Recalling now why I saved the dusty *National Geographic*, I open it, and am sure enough struck dumb by a Hubble photo even grander than that of the Orion Nebula.

To capture this image, the telescope was aimed, as the astronomers describe it, at one of the darkest parts of space, focused on an interstellar region "the size of a grain of sand held at arm's length," and 276 exposures were taken over ten days "to gather as much distant light as possible." The result is a photograph not of layers of stars, but layers of *galaxies*, literally thousands of them in this single image, stretching "as far as the Hubble's eye can see."

I walk slowly back through this. Here is a mere *speck* of our universe, a sand-size grain of it, yet when a 276-exposure jury delivers its verdict, the grain is seen to contain a vast field of jeweled galaxies glittering in blankness and blackness. The physical gaze of this photo has penetrated so deep it is not only astronomical, it's profoundly spiritual. Telling a story too vast for thought or words, here it sits on a page, speaking a beyond-language of spheres, swirls, colors, innumerable lights. Even the tiniest points in this image, the astronomers say, are not stars but entire galaxies. The light from some of them, traveling at

186,000 miles per second, takes *11 billion years* to reach Earth. This is what I call *a Roadless Area!* This is true Wilderness. The number of stars, star-birthing nebula clouds, solar systems, planets, moons, mineral-forms, life-forms, dead-forms implied by this single photo stops my mind and leaves me hearing music. If we could look back toward ourselves from some bright point here pictured, the entire Milky Way would be a small shining dot, our sun a nothingness lost in that dot, our Earth and selves an inconceivably brief dream within that nothingness. Yet what strikes me, what consoles and soothes me here, is the realization that our Earth is at one not with human industry, but with this fathomless multigalaxied swirl. Lacking some sci-fi fantasy such as "warp speed" that lets us travel millions of times faster than light, not a molecule of this vastness shall ever be disturbed, colonized, debated, exploited, degraded, or even touched by our curiously manipulative species. Human folly has knocked our planet's natural systems terribly out of balance, creating mass extinctions that are throwing the evolution of forms eons backward in time. But the birthing of stars, cooling of stars into planets, creation and evolution of planetary life are inexorable, and Earth will live on. It's only a speck of a species known as "terrestrial humanity" that may not. The wilderness in this photograph contains us the way a shoreless ocean contains a few billion drops. Even at our grandiose worst, we are a negligible jot of darkness in a boundlessness filled with symmetries, mysteries, and lights.

Improvisation #3: Assailed

On a five-foot shelf within reach of my desk I keep forty or so books I've read so often that their imaginative flights and insights now bleed into my own. Turning from the Hubble photos to this

shelf, my eyes alight on Annie Dillard's *For the Time Being*. Why?
I seem to remember words spoken by the book's hero, the French
paleontologist, priest, and mystic, Teilhard de Chardin, that once
left me feeling the same silent music I feel in these spring snow
clouds and Hubble images. I page through the book until the inner
music and Teilhard's words fuse:

> *By means of all created things, without exception, the divine
> assails us, penetrates us, and molds us. We imagined it as
> distant and inaccessible, whereas in fact we live steeped in
> its burning layers.*

These sentences somehow reverse the Hubble image, throwing
the swirl of galaxies into my interior. I'm instantly covered, head
to toe, in goosebumps. It seems an unnecessary act of cosmic
exhibitionism when, out the window, sunlight bursts forth again,
finches, crossbills, grosbeaks, and siskins burst into song, and
now blindingly bright snowflakes keep swirling down. Turning
from snow to galaxies to embryonic pink stars to a desk photo
of my daughters at age five and seven, I am assailed. Both girls
wear expressions of unusual seriousness, and our youngest, in
the photo, holds a single petal of a living sunflower. The same
flower's blind eye followed the sun across the sky every day last
summer, then in autumn bowed its head low, and in winter fed its
great single eye to the birds. The birds repaid it by hiding bits of
eye in the earth. Tiny green sprouts now unfurl all over our yard.
The sun for which the self-sacrificing flower is named is burning
four million tons of itself per second to enliven this world of birds,
sprouting life, and melting snow. Aged suns explode like old

blossoms, their fragments scattering, falling into orbits, becoming planets. The seeds of future suns gestate in fiery phallus clouds.

This sunlit snow is a falling Milky Way. The cells of my body are another. We are born of and fed by a sacrificial burning. We live steeped in its layers. My daughters' brown eyes burn serenely, yet they burn. The music of Teilhard's words rises. Tears rise. I turn from stars to sunlight to sunflowers to snow to my children's faces and feel us steeping in the sacrificial layers.

Improvisation #4: Science & Reverence
I consider the infinite wilds to be the divine manuscript, the only unbowdlerized copy we have of the Book that gives and sustains our lives. Human industry is shredding this gift like an Enron document. There are those who call the shredding "free market economics" or even "freedom." But the freedom to shred the divine manuscript is not an economics any lover of neighbor, self, or Earth wishes to practice. Once self-forgetfulness and self-giving start to give back joy, one grows bewildered by the worship of selfishness, chucks the politics of self-interest, and casts about for less suicidal hopes.

A new source of hope for me: the growing reverence for nature and its mind-bending mysteries, among scientists. This reverence marks a significant change of consciousness: The sciences, until recently, were committed to mechanistic paradigms and an obsession with the physically measurable that made reverence possible only by disconnecting spiritual realities and scientific thought. The so-called "Enlightenment" and its empirical thinking led, sans spirit, to the effective naming of things, cataloging of things, dissecting, extracting, and reconstruction of things, creating the modern world as we pretended for a time to "know it." By the late twentieth century, science divorced from spirituality had led to the genetic warping of living things; to raping, monoculturizing, and extirpating entire species of living things; to the devastating delusion that financial entities such as banks and corporations are living things; and finally to droves of humans so cosmologically lost, so buried in abstraction that they have removed humanity itself from the great tapestry of living things and granted themselves permission to treat a small fragile planet like an "infinite resource" to be plundered at will.

I see two chief causes for the countering outburst of reverence in science — one famous, one infamous. The famous cause: the new physics. Quantum mechanics has changed the way we see the universe. The old proton/neutron/electron atom is now as unfit for describing matter as is a typewriter unfit for searching the Web. Atomic particles are now believed to derive from immaterial wave packets; space is said to have had ten original dimensions that collapsed, at the beginning of time, to form the superstrings of which subatomic particles consist. Field theory; wave mechanics; morphogenesis; the recently discovered tunneling of electrons through neutrons: through a multitude of images and equations, physics now tells us that the scientific trinity of Space, Time, and Matter derive from a source infinitely subtler than all three.

The infamous cause of the new reverence in science: suffering and loss. How many biologists, botanists, ethnologists, anthropologists have been forced to renounce their fields in midcareer because their living objects of study have died out before their eyes? How many more have been so assailed by the world's barrios, war zones, biological dead zones, disease zones, oil war zones, slave labor zones that they've abandoned their discipline to become peace activists or humanitarians? I'm not going to belabor these massive problems, but I touch on them to introduce a sentence that strikes me as pivotal: humanity's greatest problems, said Albert Einstein, "cannot be solved at the same level of consciousness that created them." What is most needed in our time, he believed, is not just a dedication to problem solving, but a change in the level of human consciousness itself.

That eminently practical man, E. F. Schumacher, appears to have agreed with Einstein. Though famed for a problem-solving masterpiece on appropriate technologies, *Small Is Beautiful*, Schumacher ended his career with *A Guide for the Perplexed* — a metaphysical tour de force on human levels of consciousness and how to raise them. It strikes me in this context that among us are people in whom humanity's problems have been largely solved, people who, like Teilhard, experience the divine "assailing, penetrating and molding" them — for a person being so molded is not living at a level of consciousness capable of shredding the divine manuscript in the name of an abstracted, inhuman, biologically inert "freedom" that is in truth a license to kill.

Einstein, Schumacher, Teilhard, and others like them make me wonder what would happen if would-be problem solvers focused less exclusively on the problems coming at them? These three men were renowned for the daydreamy, highly intuitive, walkabout states in which their greatest insights came to them. I sense more here than a quirk shared by brainy eccentrics. What if our primary focus became the spirit in which we greet the dawn, our every breath, our self-sacrificial burning, and out of this reverie we turn to face our problems?

Improvisation #5: Toward Living Language

The human brain is the most complex physical object in the known universe. Its 10 billion neurons, says scientist Gerald Edelman, can make a million billion interconnections. Our thoughts and dreams fire lucidly or weave drunkenly through our cortexes in patterns as complex as stars gyring through a galaxy. Yet Sir John Carew Eccles, the Nobel Prize–winning brain researcher, tells us that the brain is not itself the cause or source of its own synaptic activity. The brain doesn't *produce* energies: It only receives them. Picking up invisible impulses, it transposes them into data the ego-consciousness can translate, but the energies themselves, says Eccles, come from a realm inaccessible to any known method of measurement. If the lexicon of science is to reflect these kinds of mysteries, the direction in which some of the world's best minds keep suggesting we travel appears to be into an ever-greater subtlety we could so worse than refer to as "spiritual."

The Benedictine contemplative, Father Willigis Jäger, in his book *Search for the Meaning of Life*, describes many convergences between the new physics and metaphysics. The micro electromagnetic forces known as L-fields, for instance, create, inform, and sustain literally everything in nature. Yet they are not a chemical process, not a mechanical sequence, not anything that pre-1960s scientific models ever described or believed in. L-fields, say those who study them, literally sculpt us and all life-forms, yet they're not "literal" at all. They're intangible. To even explain how they're detected requires a treatise more reminiscent of Saint Thomas Aquinas than Sir Isaac Newton.

Moving further into the transrational: morphogenetic fields are called metafields for the same reason metaphysics is called metaphysics. These fields are "above" (*meta*) the material realm, and can be neither seen nor measured. Indeed, in the words of scientist Rupert Sheldrake, they are "free of matter and energy" entirely! Yet morphogenetic fields, Sheldrake and others say, "shape and direct the entire animate and inanimate creation." When, for instance, a cut sprig of willow is jammed into the ground and watered, matterless, energyless morphogenetic forces from *outside the matter and energy of the sprig* cause an entire tree to grow from the cutting. Likewise, when a dragonfly egg is tied off in the middle, unseen fields from outside the egg cause an entire insect to grow from each of the two halves.

With these kinds of discoveries, we appear, in my view, to have entered another True Wilderness. Though we're still studying science, we now stand amid energyless, matterless, invisible powers that "shape and direct the entire animate and inanimate creation," and these powers are no more graspable than the contents of those Hubble-glimpsed galaxies 11 billion light-years away. I'm not trying to deify morphogenetic fields. What interests me here is the fact that I'm speaking of things beyond my comprehension—but beyond scientific comprehension as well. There is something poignant in this to me. Imaginative writers and contemplatives are used to the company of things beyond comprehension. Many scientists are not. Is there anything we more experienced Uncomprehenders can do to help these scientists feel more comfortable with swimming in the end of the pool where you never touch bottom?

That all things are shaped by fields that are *beyond energy and matter* is now what we must oxymoronically yet truthfully call "solid science." As a result, in the realm of language the scientific facts of our physical situation are becoming almost impossible to express in spiritually neutral terms. Science has moved in a generation from the easily stated but mistaken claim that we are mortal matter, chemical compounds, electrical impulses, and little more, to the inspiring but linguistically problematic claim that we are living repositories of the invisible wisdom of primordial electromagnetic and morphogenetic fields. Many scientists who disdain religion, or worse, *mysticism*, seem horrified by the mounting pressure to deploy overtly spiritual terms such as Jäger, Teilhard, and Schumacher use. But the use of such terms does not mean you've turned into a fundamentalist trying to cure contemporary plagues with the bird killings and bloody house washings of Leviticus 14.

And what of science's own pet terms? It is no more defensible, empirically speaking, to believe in a universe created by the Big Bang than in one created by Shiva's lingam. "The Big Bang was not big, it was sub-atomic," writes Sara Maitland. "And it was not a bang, it was necessarily silent, since in the absence of time and atmosphere there was nothing to convey sound waves, and nothing to receive them either." I've read definitions of quarks, muons, and subatomic waves that sound less grounded than certain definitions of the Holy Ghost. My advice to scientists in regard to this is: if unseen fields beyond literary or scientific expression lie at the root of all life-forms and matter—if these fields are invisible yet deducible, ineffable yet artful, evasive yet omnipresent, and if in the attempt to describe them science has never sounded so much like ancient myth or scripture—so be it. I realize that to many an old-school scientist, the words "ancient myth and scripture" translate to "superstitious pap." But is this anything more than arrogance? Ancient thought as expressed in wisdom literature is unanswerably profound and poetic, and great scientists who study the ancients know this. Many physicists, Robert Oppenheimer among them, have closely pondered India's five-thousand-year-old Upanishads, stunned by its exacting observations of how unseen fields and mayavic forces create and dissolve this world of forms. If it is a kind of ancient poetry that physics and fields are revealing to us, it's time our best scientists open their minds to such poetry. If our problems cannot be solved at the same level of consciousness that created them, it's time we contemplatives, scientists, writers, artists, teachers, activists, and Earth lovers transcend petty discomfiture, acclimatize to more intuitive ways of being, join forces, and bring a great reverence for the Unseen to bear on how we behave toward the seen.

Einstein: *In the new physics, there is no place for both field and matter, because field is the only reality.*

Willigis Jäger: *There aren't two kinds of laws: matter and mind. Rather, there is a single continuous law for both matter and mind. Matter is the domain of space in which the field is extremely dense.*

Teilhard de Chardin: *Concretely speaking, there is no matter and spirit. There exists only matter that is becoming spirit.*

Frederick Sommer: *Spirit is the behavior of matter. Perception does not take spiritedness into a state of affairs that does not already have it.*

Charles Darwin: *Each living creature (is) . . . a little universe, formed of a host of self-propagating organisms, inconceivably minute and as numerous as the stars in heaven.*

William Blake: *For every Space larger than a red Globule of Man's blood / is visionary . . . And every Space smaller than a Globule of Man's blood, / open into Eternity of which this vegetable Earth is but a shadow.*

Lord Krishna: *Behind the manifest and unmanifest there is an Existence that is eternal and changeless. This Existence is not dissolved in the general cosmic dissolution. Fools pass blindly by it, and of its majesty know nothing. It is nearer than knowing. . . . Having been, it will never not be; unborn, enduring, constant, primordial, it is not killed when the body is killed. . . . Weapons do not cut it, fire does not burn it, waters do not wet it, wind does not wither it.*

Stephen Hawking: *What is it that breathes fire into the equations and makes a universe for them to describe?*

John of the Cross: *The fire! The fire inside!*

Living science.

Improvisation #6: Beyond-Language

The word *mysticism* was unknown to me as a boy. My child mind excelled at acceptance, declined categorization, embraced spirit, matter, and contradictions without preference or judgment, and everything that happened simply was.

The word *mysticism* still means little to me as an experiencer, because all that I experience continues to simply be what it is, and no modifier changes that. But as a writer in love with a world in which much of what is visible is being assaulted with extreme violence and much of what is life-giving is unseen, I confess to being the beneficiary of certain inner/outer cusp experiences that became beacons in my life, and admit that my respect for the word *mysticism* grows if only because, by definition, it shepherds us toward realms in which "what is" is much more than merely physical in the inert and abstracted sense foisted upon us by the creators of industrial havoc. I am therefore stepping, this fine March day in my fiftieth year, out of a closet in which I've spent my life happily hidden, and openly confessing myself (with a blue-collar, rednecked blush) to be the experiential mystic I have always been.

My lifelong love of rivers is partly responsible. In visiting the same streams year in and year out as Earth tilts on her axis, causing foliage, insects, fish, birds, seasons to arrive out of a seeming nowhere, things occasionally tilt on some kind of interior axis, causing invisible yet artful, imperceptible yet detectable forces to arrive out of a seeming nowhere in me. I have mostly used fiction as a repository for these unexpected falls into inwardness. But as I grow older, I notice the way great nature-probing nonfictioneers— including the Williams Blake and Wordsworth, Emerson, Dickinson, Whitman, Muir, Jeffers, Borges, Merton, Akhmatova, Gary Snyder, W. S. Merwin, Wendell Berry, Jack Gilbert, Annie Dillard, Pattiann Rogers, Mary Oliver, Jane Hirshfield, Ursula K. Le Guin, and innumerably more, unapologetically leap now and then in their writing, as they leap in their lives, from discursive language and the outer world into "beyond-language" and inner realms. Friendship with several people in this list and immersion in the natural world have convinced me: These linguistic leaps are almost all based on simple fidelity to experience. When experience flies into realms that language cannot touch, honesty demands *beyond-language*.

Consider Henry David Thoreau. In a letter to one H.G.O. Blake, Thoreau avers that humans freed of all self-limitation can participate in the same kind of creative acts as the Creator: "Free in this world as the birds in the air, disengaged from every kind of chains, those who have practiced the yoga gather in Brahma the certain fruit of their works. . . . The yogi, absorbed in contemplation, contributes in his degree to creation: he breathes a divine perfume, he hears wonderful things. Divine forms traverse

him without tearing him, and, united to the nature which is proper
to him, he goes, he acts as animating original matter. . . . Depend
upon it that, rude and careless as I am, I would fain practice the
yoga faithfully."

Although my reason struggles with what Henry is saying here,
my intuition is struck by this:

Thoreau: *Divine forms traverse him without tearing him* . . .

Teilhard: *The divine assails us, penetrates us, molds us* . . .

What sort of experiences create such similar sentences?

Though famed for an astute midwestern groundedness, Aldo
Leopold too leapt, now and then, from natural history into mystical
testimony. In *A Sand County Almanac* he wrote:

> *The song of a river ordinarily means the tune that waters play*
> *on rock, root, and rapid. . . . This song of the waters is audible*
> *to every ear, but there is other music in these hills, by no means*
> *audible to all. To hear even a few notes of it you must first live*
> *here for a long time, and you must know the speech of hills and*
> *rivers. Then on a still night, when the campfire is low and the*
> *Pleiades have climbed over rimrocks, sit quietly and listen for a*
> *wolf to howl, and think hard of everything you have seen and*
> *tried to understand. Then you may hear it—a vast, pulsing*
> *harmony—its score inscribed on a thousand hills, its notes the*
> *lives and deaths of plants and animals, its rhythms spanning*
> *the seconds and the centuries.*

Reason attacks such assertions. "A thousand hills!" it huffs. "Is
this *science*? Is Aldo's *vast harmony* supposedly audible? Then why
can't *I* hear it? And how can he claim to have heard something that

spans centuries when he himself died in less than a century? This is
a buncha late-night campfire *woowoo*. His editors should've cut it."

Reason makes all such leaps sound foolish, because they
are foolish—to unadorned reason. But from boyhood through
manhood it has been my experience that trying to grasp an insight,
a deep mystery, a transrational experience, or any act of love via
reason alone is rather like trying to play a guitar with one's butt.
Our reason, like our butt, is a tremendously important part of
us—but not for the purpose of hearing "vast pulsing harmonies."
As E. F. Schumacher puts it, "Nothing can be perceived without an
appropriate organ of perception."

Reason does not perceive the transrational. This is not to demean
it. It's only to say that, unless trained like a bird dog to heel in
the presence of love and mystery, reason lunges forth barking
and frantically charging, scaring off metameanings that only the
heart could have hoped to embrace. When a superb reasoner
like Teilhard says that "the divine assails us, penetrates us, and
molds us," he has not left his sanity behind: only his reason. He
is exposing matter to spirit. He's using beyond-language to do it.
We can choose to journey with him. Our reason can't. The notion
that we can stand apart from all things, can infer the existence
and true properties of all things, and can solve the dire problems
we've created for ourselves with reason alone, is what I would call
rationalist *woowoo*.

In the medieval contemplative classic *The Cloud of Unknowing*,
the anonymous author states that "no evil can touch, and no
reasoning make an impact upon, the divine creativity that proceeds
from the depths of the soul." Spiritually speaking, nothing's
changed since those words were set down. And the same words can

be said of the symphony of forces woven through galaxies, unseen fields, synapses, ecosystems, subatomic particles, and cells. The physical universe, as we now understand it, cannot be accurately described via static or boxed-in modes of thought, for that which enlivens all things is dynamic, imperceptible, limitless, and—I believe with all the science of my heart—*holy*. We are steeped in and assailed by this holiness even as we attempt to study it. We have no objective distance from it and never shall.

Improvisation #7: Music of the Spheres
Another Teilhard declaration Annie Dillard cited in *For the Time Being*. "It is precisely because he is so infinitely profound and punctiform that God is infinitely near."

The first time I read this I had no idea what it meant, so I looked up the word *punctiform*. Seldom has a dictionary had a more powerful effect: the instant I knew that punctiform means "of the nature of a point or dot," Teilhard's sentence smote me with yearning. I still understood nothing, but my memory and intuition sensed something incredible. Tying my dog, Reason, by its leash to a figurative tree, I crept up on possible metameanings without it.

Pondering Teilhard's sentence, Annie asks, "Is it useful and wise to think of God as punctiform?" This question sounded so odd and rhetorical to me that I expected a joke to follow. When instead Annie wrote, "I think so," chills ran up and down my spine.

Next she cited a scientific study of sand, of all things, informing us that the oldest grains of sand on Earth are the most perfectly spherical, and that a river takes a million years to move a spheroid grain a mere hundred miles.

Back at the tree, Reason howled, "What's any of that got to do with anything? Who can claim to even know such a thing? These supposed observers of Earth are no longer *on* Earth! They're lost in space! And now you've tied me to a fuckin' tree and are wandering off with *them!* Come back here! Untie me! You *need* me!"

I answered Reason like so: "Sit. Stay. And ponder how you ever could have claimed to *know* your nonexistent old proton/neutron/electron atoms? I know that I need you—to do stuff like my taxes. But there's something singing inside me and I want to hear it and your racket buries the music. So take a rest."

Reason sank into a sulk. The rest of me sank into reflection:

It is precisely because he is so infinitely profound and punctiform that God is infinitely near.

Why did Teilhard's references to "the nature of a point or dot" and "nearness" smote me with yearning? Why did Annie answer Teilhard with the crazy fact, *The oldest grains of sand on Earth are the most perfectly spherical?* Why did that fact sing inside me?

Sitting quiet with these questions—not trying to answer them, just enjoying their company—I suddenly fell through a floor inside myself and landed amid a recurring late childhood experience. To speak of such a thing is to speak of a mystery intelligible to me only as mystery. I have no language with which to approach this experience but *beyond-language*. I know before writing of it that my description will leave me sounding like a fool to my reason, and to many readers. But I'm not getting any younger. The thought of dying without having described this mystery makes me feel like an ingrate. I prefer fools to ingrates, and try to live, act, and write accordingly. I'm not alone. In the thirteenth century Jalal al-Din Rumi spoke a spontaneous poem in

Persian, which poem a disciple set down, scholars later translated into English, and the contemporary poet Coleman Barks refined to sound like this:

> *Don't go to sleep one night.*
> *What you most want will*
> *come to you then. Warmed*
> *by a sun inside, you'll see*
> *wonders. Tonight, don't put*
> *your head down. Be tough,*
> *and strength will come.*
> *That which adoration adores*
> *appears at night.*

Late in boyhood, but lasting into manhood, I had a recurring experience of what Aldo Leopold might call *a vast, pulsing harmony* and Teilhard *an infinite punctiformity*. Beginning when I was eleven or twelve—always after long, vigorous days spent wandering outdoors—I'd lie down in the dark, so dazzled by the day's wonders that I would consciously swear off sleep and keep pondering all I'd seen and done. While conducting these reviews I eventually entered a state wherein my body felt as though it was pleasantly vibrating and my eyes began to see in a waking dark. What normally followed this state was a fall into dream, then sleep. My trick, however, was to fiercely resist that falling and keep gazing at whatever my state let me see. I would "be tough," as Rumi advised. And sure enough, strength would come.

The beyond-language experience began when the vibration of my body was joined by an exquisite sense of density, of massive physical weight. This weight felt vastly greater and *other* than the weight of my body: it seemed a physical visitation by something heavy and huge, something a physicist might choose to call "a field." The only reason the weight didn't crush me, it seemed, was that it permeated me the way colors permeate our seeing, or water permeates a sponge: I grew so absorbed by "the field" that there was no "me" to crush.

Soon after the density grew palpable, I heard an oceanic hum: a single note, majestically deep and simple. To hear this note annihilated desire. The sound was so beautiful it was impossible to want to hear more. Any question I might have asked about who or what made it, where it came from, how it was produced, felt answered without speaking by the great hum itself.

Simultaneous to the sound, I saw—as plainly as I'd seen the light and objects of the day—an enormous sphere. This sphere, I knew instantly, was the source of the music, the density, the massive weight. It floated in a sea of black. I hovered before it, its motionless satellite, though once the experience began, pronouns became impossible: "I" was now an invisible perceiver consisting of the senses of feeling, hearing, and sight. Body and mind were gone. *Being* continued to do just fine without them.

The enormous sphere was a swirling mass of reds and oranges, lit from within, vast as a close-up star, though not at all hot. My being pulsed in tune with its massive hum, a sensation indescribably blissful, yet peaceful. Fear and excitement were not possible in this musical state. There was no ego to excite, no body to be afraid for. The sphere was not only the *largest* thing in existence, it was the *only* thing in existence, and to watch, to feel, to hear it replaced "me" with a state I can only call *selfless adoration*. And the experience grew richer. Adoration of the sphere had movements, like a symphony, and every time the movements were the same:

First Movement: After adoring the sphere for a time, adoration would move toward it with a sense of enormous anticipation, until the sphere's dimensions seemed impossibly vast, its note capable of singing a universe into existence, but all gentle despite its infinite potency. When selfless adoration could approach no closer, the intimacy was as delicate as when we touch, with a cautious fingertip, the surface tension of still water. Adoration remained on one side of this tension. *Infinitely profound and punctiform, infinitely near,* the sphere's music, light, and power reigned on the other.

Second Movement: When proximity to the sphere could not be closer, selfless adoration experienced a thrill something like when a jet plane hits an air pocket and drops a thousand feet, only not frightening, and it suddenly became possible to see, feel, and hear in the opposite direction from that in which adoration had been gazing. What it beheld brought bliss:

A second sphere had been born. The very twin of the first. Precisely as magnificent. Precisely as vast and profoundly close. The oceanic hum had also doubled. The discovery of the second sphere sent *cataclysms* of pleasure through me. (I'm trying hard to avoid sexual terms here.) An orb so vast it seemed all-encompassing had divided like a cell, creating a second all-encompassingness. Lodged between them, selfless perception turned one way, then the other, adoring them both.

Third Movement: Anticipation rose again. Selfless adoration backed away from the two vast spheres until they could be seen in their entirety, and they divided like cells again, this time *visibly*, creating four of themselves, and fourfold bliss, their oceanic

hum a fourfold harmony now. The plot thickened, grew fruitful,
multiplied. The spheres created 8 of themselves, then 16, 32, 64,
128, every orb glowing, lit from within, the music, sense of blissful
density and mass, coming in waves, *a vast, pulsing harmony.* They
loved to divide; loved to be fruitful. At each division, the de-selfed
adoration "I" had become felt their love as its very own. Awash in
this geometrical, musical mode, adoration watched the spheres go
on dividing, grow incalculable in number, pour forth color, hum
their multitudinous song, till they were so numerous that adoration
had to draw away to behold them all. Still dividing, still self-
generating, they gradually came to look like a vast wall of spheroid
fruits, growing smaller with each division—first melons, then
grapefruits, then oranges, apricots, wrong-colored grapes, then
blueberries, then currants, then tiny seeds, the something even
smaller, say, a vast field of singing, internally lit grains of sand. (*The
oldest grains of sand are the most perfectly spherical.*)

Final Movement: The infinity of now microscopic spheres kept
halving till they could no longer remain separate; they divided into
an infinity of grains so minute they lost their particularity and
merged back into a single vast unity, their countless harmonies
merged into the original, single basso profundo note, selfless
adoration returned, with a swoon of bliss, to being an I, and
I realized I was back in the Beginning, gazing at the smooth,
infinitely punctiform surface of the Original Vast Sphere, floating
in a sea of black, me hovering before it in a state I can only call
adoration. And the entire "symphony" commenced, movement by
movement, exactly as before, a second time, sometimes a third,
until I fell asleep in an exhaustion of density, division, creation,
music, and bliss.

Improvisation #8: Fruits

There it is: a mystery intelligible to me only as mystery. And to this day I don't know beans about the "meaning" or "utility" of the experience. Such experiences don't care if they're comprehensible, useful, apropos, politic, polite: such experiences *assail*. But I've always loved and trusted the line: *By their fruits ye shall know them.* And in applying it to the spheres I realize that, mysterious as they remain, they *have* created tangible fruits.

When, for instance, I first heard of medieval cosmologists referring to a "music of the spheres," my faithful dog Reason howled even as the heart of me felt, *Yes!* And when I first found the Vedic description of a state in which the soul perceives infinite hugeness and infinite smallness as one and the same, and the Koranic statement, "All Creation in the hands of the Merciful One is smaller than a mustard seed," I again felt, *Of course!* And when I learned of the mathematician Georg Cantor proving that infinities come in an infinite range of sizes, and read Paul Davies's discussion of Cantor ("Any absolute, being a Unity and hence complete within itself, must include itself"), I thought: *Beautiful Spheres, Final Movement.*

And when I opened the dusty *National Geographic* this morning, saw galaxies swirling in a jot of universe "the size of a grain of sand held at arm's length," and Teilhard's words on punctiformity and nearness flipped these galaxies into a vast interior, my eyes filled because, for a timeless moment, I heard the profundo hum of a glorious old nighttime companion. And when I dreamed, just the other night, that I was shot dead by a hundred machine guns, shot so many times that a dark bullet-driven wind blew my soul irrevocably away from my dead body and I was invisible and afraid

and had neither breath nor voice with which to call out to my God,
I called out in bodiless desperation anyway, and a spheric and
punctiform point pierced the grim field in which I drifted, the point
expanded, tore that gray world's wall apart like so much wet tissue,
light poured through, and I saw the Beloved's cheek and brilliant
eye peeking at me through the hole, just that much of Him, yet
there was such love in that eye, such *What-a-trick-I've-pulled!* glee,
that a posthumous existence without need of this soon-to-be-former
body felt not just possible but certain and I woke with a jolt of joy.
And when, in searching for Teilhard's "assailed" sentence this
morning, I reread Annie:

> *There is no less holiness at this time—as you are reading*
> *this—than there was the day the Red Sea parted. . . . There*
> *is no whit less might in heaven or on earth than there was*
> *the day Jesus said, "Maid, arise" to the centurion's daughter,*
> *or the day Peter walked on water, or the night Mohammed*
> *flew to heaven on a horse. . . . In any instant you may avail*
> *yourself of the power to love your enemies; to accept failure,*
> *slander, or the grief of loss; or to endure torture. . . . "Each*
> *and every day the Divine Voice issues from Sinai," says the*
> *Talmud. Of eternal fulfillment, Tillich said, "If it is not seen*
> *in the present, it cannot be seen at all."*

I felt nothing but an urge to shout: *Go Annie! You're singin' the*
spheric gospel now!

The sensations of weight, of palpable presence, of *hum*, still
come over me now and again walking in cities and mountains,
wading through traffic or trout streams. I don't consciously seek

such sensations; they just check in, now and then, in the course
of what comes. A spring aspen leaf might brush my face, and
I close my eyes and find myself feeling the tiny, self-contained
universe that is a spring-green aspen cell suddenly dividing
into two of itself, and thus growing, *because it loves to*. I witness
"fruitful multiplication" in our Montana-winter-blighted fruit
trees, the year's brood of bantam chicks, the creeks' insects or river
bottoms' whitetail fawns, the newborn wood ducks, kingfishers,
killdeers, and wonder comes upon me as the densities, unions
and divisions of love grow palpable. I've stood by the ocean at the
Columbia River's mouth, seen the subtle curve of horizon, felt the
oceans' sevenfold hum, and seen the seas as a single sphere. I've
had the sense, standing in running water, that I've been not just
close to the molecules flowing round me but *inside* them; that I've
experienced, in the womb or eons earlier, the coming together and
breaking apart of spheric particles of H and of O. I've witnessed
plants, animals, family, friends migrating or transmigrating to
places known or unknown; felt us jolt into newborn awarenesses
or out of old bodies; witnessed our slow, sure breakdown by
organic or industrial attrition, and equally sure transformations of
matter, energy, soul, as the *thousand hills* feeling and a vast pulsing
harmony fill every grain of us with anguished joy.

It's time I stopped building sentences now and stepped down to
the creek, as I've done half my life, early evenings. This time of year
I'll look for the rainbow trout that migrate up from the larger rivers
to spawn. And I'll find a pair, if this spring is like the last eight,
in a tiny side channel a quarter mile downstream. As I approach
them on my belly, I'll be crawling across spheroid grains of white
granitic sand, then lying prostrate, achieving *nearness*, watching a

female an arm's length from my eyes beat her body against cobble, build a stone nest, and fill it with a thousand lit-from-within orange spheres. I'll watch the male ease over like one of the dark snow clouds that passed over all day, and when the milt pours down, each nested sphere will suddenly love to divide and divide until it's a sphere no longer, but a needle-size sphere-eyed fish. I'll encounter the same troutlings over the slow course of coming summers, drifting down toward the rivers, growing by dividing, defeating time; I'll catch them now and then, release most, eat a few, and the survivors will return in twelve or sixteen seasons bearing the milt clouds, lit spheres, and hidden fields that carry the genius of trout toward my children's children's world.

There's not much more to discuss here. Either I'm crazy or I'm not, and the kingdom of heaven is within us or it isn't, and a divine punctiformity exists or it doesn't, and we sense it or we don't. If we do, God help us, and if we don't, God help us, because if inner kingdoms and morphogenetic truth are delusions, where's the harm? You think Congress isn't deluded? If the punctiform spheres I've glimpsed are delusions, then Congress, the spheres, and I are three phantasms amid a chaos of delusions and one phantasm is as good or bad as another, so hey ho!, let's sally forth in the most ginormous internally combusting phantasm-mobiles possible and purchase only the choicest consumer delusions till the galaxies abort us, amen.

But if the punctiformities I've glimpsed in some sense *do* exist—if each and every day the Divine Voice *does* issue from Sinai, and every inch of Creation is pierced by its song and every dot point cell particle field is so moved by the Music that it loves to sing swell divide transform and bear all fruit and all life and all death and all

regeneration in response—well then *ahhhh!* How grateful I am to
be here! And how carefully and attentively I want to live!

I still have no rational idea what it *means* when consciousness
revs up and perceives unanswerable mystery amid life and matter.
But oh do I have *images* of what it means! I can't lend rational
credence to Annie's sense that punctiformity is "helpful in sensing
God." But I can lend a little beyond-credence. If we are ever to rise
to new levels of consciousness or to the Beauty that is Truth, we've
got to describe our perceptions as consciousness truly perceives
them. I therefore confess my lifelong love for a wilderness found
outside myself until, once in a precious while, it appears within.
It's a wilderness entered, it seems, through agendaless alertness at
work, rest, or play in the presence of language, rivers, mountains,
music, plants, creatures, rocks, moon, sun, dust, pollen grains,
dots, spheres, galaxies, grains of sand, stars, cells, DNA, molecules,
atomic particles, and immaterial forces. It's a wilderness that,
rather than out me as a damn fool mystic, "inside-outs" me,
leading to the adoration of a Teilhardinian burning and Leopoldian
harmony that leave my mind wondrously happy but far, far behind.
It's a wilderness my trusty dog, Reason, will never succeed in
sniffing out and chomping up, yet a wilderness I've been so long
and gratefully assailed by that I've lost all but comic interest in
the dog's endless hounding and suspect even he begins to enjoy
himself when the wilderness flips us inside itself.

I believe—based on phallic clouds giving birth to stars, spring
storm clouds to snow, summer snowbanks to rivers, orange orbs
to trout; I believe based on punctiform dots melting into the
vastest sphere imaginable, then dividing its way back into dots;
I believe based on lives collapsing into ashes and dust, dust and

ashes bursting back to life, and spheric shapes dividing just as cells divide, creating all plants, all creatures, children, sunflowers, sun, and self by sacrificing all that they are to be reconfigured and reborn forever—that when we feel Love's density, see its colors, feel its hum or pulse, it's time to quit reason and cry: "*My God! Thanks!*" If I stake my life on one field, one wild force, one sentence issuing from Sinai, it is this one: *There is no goal beyond love.*

PATTIANN ROGERS

Romance

In love with the body, especially when
it dances in love with its own dance as it toes
and taps . . . flickers, creepers, chickadees
around a tree trunk, a click beetle in a flipping
somersault, the soft-shoe swish and sway
of the chee and feather grasses, the lissom uvas;

in love with the melding of the body,
especially when it languishes in the surf
of its own sleep . . . the belly slump of a leopard
stretched high on a branch, camouflaged,
leaf and fur, the tight sleep of a tumblebug egg
in its buried pod of dung, the man in a backyard
hammock slowly rocking with the slowly
rolling sun through evening shadows;

(so floats the sea otter on its back, bobbing
with the rocking sea, so bobs the gelatinous
umbrella and stinging strings of the jellyfish,
jelly and sting being the design and event
of the sea's own rolling body)

especially when the perfumes of a vigorous
body at rest are of the salt of the sea, his body
itself being the salt of the earth, in love
with the taste when the salt is tasted;

no ardor surpasses a body on the hunt,
halting abruptly, one foot lifted above the snow,
poised, as intent as frozen air, eyes as pure
and sharp as ice, then the bolt—the *élancé*—
beat and soul wholly in pursuit—the sail—
the contact—most foreign, most familiar,
on the far edge of the horizon.

BIOGRAPHIES

A. R. Ammons (1926–2001) was an award-winning poet and professor at Cornell University. "Love Song" is from *The Complete Poems of A. R. Ammons: Volume 1 1955–1977*, edited by Robert M. West. Used by permission of W. W. Norton & Company.

Ellen Bass is a chancellor of the Academy of American Poets. She is the author of many poetry collections, including *Like a Beggar* and *The Human Line*. Her newest book, *Indigo*, will be published by Copper Canyon Press in 2020.

Traci Brimhall is the author of the poetry collections *Saudade, Our Lady of the Ruins*, and *Rookery*. Her children's book, *Sophia & the Boy Who Fell*, was published by SeedStar Books in March 2017.

Tom Crawford (1939–2018) was the author of nine books of poetry. "Prayer" appeared in *The Temple on Monday* and *The Names of Birds*. Reprinted with the permission of Eastern Washington University Press, Sherman Asher Publishing, and the estate of Tom Crawford.

Deborah DeNicola is the author of six books, most recently *Original Human*.

Natalie Diaz was born and raised in the Fort Mojave Indian Village in Needles, California. She is the author of the poetry collection *When My Brother Was an Aztec.* "Wolf OR-7" will appear in her new collection, *Postcolonial Love Poem.* Reprinted with permission of Graywolf Press.

Duy Doan is the author of *We Play a Game,* winner of the 2017 Yale Series of Younger Poets Prize. A Kundiman fellow, he received an MFA from Boston University.

David James Duncan is the author of the novels *The River Why* and *The Brothers K,* the story collection *River Teeth,* the nonfiction collection *My Story as Told by Water,* and most recently *God Laughs and Plays.*

Camille Dungy's most recent books are *Trophic Cascade* and *Guide-book to Relative Strangers.*

James Galvin has published seven books of poems and two prose works. He teaches at the Iowa Writers' Workshop.

Lance Garland's adventure series, *Itinerant,* is available on Prime Reading and was a finalist for the 2019 International Book Awards for LGBT fiction.

Eva Hooker is the author of the poetry collection *Godwit.* She is professor of English and writer in residence at Saint Mary's College, Notre Dame, Indiana.

Pam Houston is the author of the memoir *Deep Creek*, the novels *Contents May Have Shifted* and *Sight Hound*, the story collections *Cowboys Are My Weakness* and *Waltzing the Cat*, and the essay collection *A Little More About Me*, all published by W. W. Norton & Company.

Cynthia Huntington is the author of the poetry collections *The Radiant, The Fish-Wife,* and *We Have Gone to the Beach,* and the nonfiction book *The Salt House*. She is a professor of English and creative writing at Dartmouth College.

Alex Carr Johnson is the Alaska Program Manager for the National Parks Conservation Association. His essay in this anthology is a revision of the original version that appeared in *Orion*.

Joseph O. Legaspi is the author of the poetry collections *Threshold* and *Imago*. He cofounded Kundiman, a nonprofit serving Asian American writers.

Gretchen Legler is the author, most recently, of *On the Ice*. She is a professor of English at the University of Maine Farmington.

Barry Lopez is the author of fourteen books, including *Arctic Dreams*, which won the National Book Award. His most recent book is *Horizon*.

Cate Lycurgus's work has appeared in *The American Poetry Review, Tin House,* and elsewhere. She lives south of San Francisco.

Teddy Macker is the author of the poetry collection *This World*. He teaches creative writing and literature at the University of California, Santa Barbara.

David Tomas Martinez is the author of the poetry collections *Post Traumatic Hood Disorder* and *Hustle*, both released by Sarabande Books.

Jean Monahan is the author of the poetry books *Hands, Believe It or Not*, and *Mauled Illusionist*.

Kathleen Dean Moore is a philosopher, environmental advocate, and writer. Her most recent book is *Great Tide Rising*. She is a Distinguished Professor of philosophy at Oregon State University, where she cofounded the Spring Creek Project for Ideas, Nature, and the Written Word.

Laurel Nakanishi is a writer and educator from Honolulu, Hawai'i. She is the author of the book of poetry *Ashore*, forthcoming from Tupelo Press.

Nick Neely is the author of *Alta California* and *Coast Range*, both released by Counterpoint Press.

Mary Rose O'Reilley taught English and environmental studies at University of St. Thomas from 1978 to 2006. She is the author of the nonfiction books *The Love of Impermanent Things* and *The Barn at the End of the World* and the poetry collections *Earth, Mercy* and *Half Wild*, the latter selected by Mary Oliver for the Walt Whitman Award.

Nathaniel Perry is the author of the poetry collection *Nine Acres*. He is an associate professor of English and editor of *The Poetry Review* at Hampden-Sydney College.

Robert Michael Pyle lives in the Columbia-Pacific region. "Carnal Knowledge" appears in *The Tangled Bank: Writings from* Orion. Reprinted with the permission of Oregon State University Press.

Jill Sisson Quinn is the author of *Deranged*. "Metamorphic" will be included in her new book, *Sign Here if You Exist*, due out in 2020 from Ohio State University Press.

Pattiann Rogers is the author of twelve collections of poetry and two collections of essays, including *Quickening Fields, The Grand Array, Firekeeper,* and *Song of the World Becoming*.

Scott Russell Sanders is the author of twenty books of fiction and nonfiction, including *A Private History of Awe* and *A Conservationist Manifesto*. Among his honors are the Lannan Literary Award and the Mark Twain Award. In 2012 he was elected to the American Academy of Arts and Sciences.

Mark Schimmoeller is the author of *Slowspoke*, a travel memoir of his time crossing the U.S. on a unicycle. He lives off the grid in Kentucky.

James Thomas Stevens is the author of six poetry collections, including *A Bridge Dead in the Water* and *Combing the Snakes from His Hair*. He is a member of the Akwesasne Mohawk Tribe.

Mark Sullivan is the author of the poetry collection *Slag*, which includes "My Love Feeds the Crows." Reprinted courtesy of Texas Tech University.

Katrina Vandenberg is the author of *The Alphabet Not Unlike the World* and *Atlas*. She is a professor in the Creative Writing Programs at Hamline University.

LOVE NOTES

In honor of my loving wife Lynda.
—Bob

Fred dearest,
Time evaporates with you. For hours, you delight in the leaves
dancing, all the shades and kinds of green you point out. You tell
me every day, you love me more than yesterday. And I say the same
to you, for as long as we have. Forever. Each moment.
Love, Linda

My Beloved
is there
ever a
before us

and i

wonder if
there might
ever be
an after
—Michael

Sometimes, maybe all the time, when the house won't settle and
there's no sleep anywhere, I tread lightly past yesterday's earplugs
and look for your warm hand in the dark.
—SP

Koren, I would marry you a fourth time. Wink.

My father had dignity. At the / end of his life his life began
to wake in me. — Sharon Olds
Miss you, Dad. And I love you.
— Tara

For SAW,
Loving you in words, and in every space between them. There
aren't new words for this, so let's repeat ourselves. Let's keep
repeating ourselves.
Yours.
GL

To Ben, and a lifetime of vert. I love you.
—Rachel

NT to KR — From Montana's Big Sky to Zanzibar, New Mexico
to New England, I'm more available than ever before to the magic
and mystery of this world because of our newfound path together.
Thank you.

Christine — I love you, I love our boy, I love our life together. I've
always been lucky, but being married to you makes me the luckiest.
Alarik

William —
I bring to you with reverent hands
All the books that my love abides.
— Madeline

More books from *Orion*

To Eat with Grace

Animals & People

Leave No Child Inside

Wonder and Other Survival Skills

Change Everything Now

Thirty-Year Plan:
Thirty Writers on What We Need
to Build a Better Future

Beyond Ecophobia:
Reclaiming the Heart
in Nature Education

Into the Field:
A Guide to Locally
Focused Learning

Place-Based Education:
Connecting Classrooms
& Communities